KILLED CARTOONS

ALSO EDITED BY DAVID WALLIS

Killed: Great Journalism Too Hot to Print

KILLED CARTOONS

CASUALTIES FROM THE WAR ON FREE EXPRESSION

EDITED BY DAVID WALLIS

W. W. NORTON & COMPANY
NEW YORK LONDON

Manufacturing by The Haddon Craftsmen, Inc.
Book design by Anna Oler

Library of Congress Cataloging-in-Publication Data

Killed cartoons : casualties from the war on free expression / edited by
David Wallis. — 1st ed.
p. cm.
ISBN-13: 978-0-393-32924-7 (pbk.)
ISBN-10: 0-393-32924-0 (pbk.)
1. United States—Politics and government—20th century—Caricatures
and cartoons. 2. United States—Politics and government—2001—Caricatures and
cartoons. 3. Editorial cartoons—United States—History. 4. Editorial cartoonists—
United States—Biography. 5. American wit and humor, Pictorial. 6. Freedom of
expression—United States—Miscellanea.
7. Censorship—United States—Case studies. I. Wallis, David.
E743.K55 2007
070.4'42—dc22   2006033191

W. W. Norton & Company, Inc.
500 Fifth Avenue, New York, N.Y. 10110
www.wwnorton.com

W. W. Norton & Company Ltd.
75/76 Wells Street, London W1T 3QT

1 2 3 4 5 6 7 8 9 0

HE WHO DARES NOT OFFEND
CANNOT BE HONEST.

—THOMAS PAINE

CONTENTS

INTRODUCTION

I'm a killer.

While compiling this collection of editorial art "killed" by newspapers and magazines because of the potential for controversy, I solicited a contribution from prominent South African cartoonist Jonathan Shapiro. In 2003, a not-for-profit organization in Cape Town asked Shapiro, who was imprisoned for six weeks during apartheid, to stage a one-man show of his cartoons. The exhibit—intended to entertain a visiting delegation of U.S. congressmen who wanted to learn about South Africa's Truth and Reconciliation Commission hearings—was cosponsored by the Faith & Politics Institute, which is based in Washington, D.C.

The institute describes its mission as providing political leaders with "occasions for moral reflection." But reflection was in short supply when the organization's director, Doug Tanner, previewed the exhibit. Some of Shapiro's caustic cartoons ridiculed the foreign policies of Presidents George W. Bush and Bill Clinton, prompting Tanner to demand the cancellation of the entire exhibit. After negotiations with the event's South

African organizers (but not with Shapiro), a compromise was struck: three of the offending cartoons were pulled from the show. Tanner later said he worried that the sight of the cartoons would have "sabotaged" his bipartisan delegation of public servants.

The story seemed a natural for this book, and I liked Shapiro's caricature of Bush as Uncle Sam giving the world the finger. But ultimately I decided that I could not publish this cartoon, because it did not meet the criterion I had established for inclusion in the book: *editorial art that had been rejected by newspapers and magazines.*

The point is that reasonable motives sometimes inspire editors to kill. The world changes so fast that a political cartoon drawn today may seem dated tomorrow; an assigning art director suddenly leaves a magazine and a successor wants to work with illustrators with whom he or she is familiar; and sometimes a promising idea just doesn't work on paper—the drawing or the writing falls flat, and the whole thrust of the cartoon is lost. Editors do, after all, play an important role in journalism. It's the editor's job to pipe up when commentators wield a blunt ax where a scalpel would be more appropriate. Editors also keep their charges from breaking libel laws, flouting journalistic ethics, and *gratuitously* offending people.

Insult should be a by-product of a reasoned argument rather than a goal in itself.

But too often editors fail to make that distinction. They suppress compelling illustrations, editorial cartoons, and political comics out of fear—fear of angering advertisers, the publisher's golf partners, the publisher's wife, the local dogcatcher, or the president of the United States, blacks, Asians, Hispanics, homophobes, gays, pro-choice advocates and antiabortion protestors alike, Catholics, Jews, Moslems, and midwestern grannies—especially midwestern grannies. They even fear getting noticed. Cartoonist Milt Priggee remembers the warning an editor gave him soon after he joined the *Spokesman-Review* in Spokane, Washington:

"If you want to survive at this paper you've gotta stay under management's radar. Don't do anything good. Don't do anything bad." ¼

Newspaper editors talk a lot about the importance of covering local issues, yet many cartoonists have received explicit warnings from management to avoid antagonizing powerful interests in their communities. J. D. Crowe, of the *Mobile Register* in Alabama, "likes to poke fun at the locals because they squirm the most," but when he worked at a paper in Fort Worth, Texas, he could not go after his local congressman, then–House Speaker Jim Wright (who later resigned his office because of financial improprieties). "We stayed away from him because he brought so much pork to our community," remembers Crowe. When Crowe joined the now-defunct *San Diego Evening Tribune*, he drew several irreverent cartoons about Mayor Maureen Frances O'Connor, a pal of the paper's publisher, Helen Copley. "My editor called me into his office and said, 'Mrs. Copley is in town . . . this week so let's play it cool.' I asked him, 'What do you mean by "playing it cool"?' He said, 'We can't talk about the mayor.' "

In-house censorship all too often keeps cartoonists from diving fists first into the middle of a public scrum. "The job of the cartoonist," Pat Oliphant once said, "is to be against the government, whatever it is. Bill Mauldin used to say, 'If it's big, hit it.' That's what we do, and if the newspapers don't back us up, there's not much future for political cartooning."

In recent years, critics inside and outside the media have decried the rise of the visual one-liner, also known as the "gag cartoon"—jokes about boob jobs and hair plugs intended to appeal to the widest possible audience. MSNBC cartoonist Daryl Cagle calls the trend "Newsweekification," referring to the magazine's tendency to run cartoons with about as much bite as a goldfish. As former *Los Angeles Times* cartoonist Paul Conrad put it to the *American Journalism Review*: "Damn few [editors] want cartoons that say something that should be said, politically, that is. As long as that continues, cartoonists are going to be in bad shape, but not as bad shape as the publishers and owners of the newspapers will be in when the people realize they're not reading anything."

Clay Bennett, of the *Christian Science Monitor*, blames the surge in lightweight cartoons on a lack of competition. He rattles off cities that have lost newspapers in the last few decades: St. Louis, Dallas, Miami, Buffalo, Pittsburgh, to name just a few. "People woke up one morning after the battle for that media market and found themselves a newspaper and a cartoonist shy," says Bennett. "You would think that the one paper standing victorious might [be] emboldened to be more aggressive—it's the only game in town—but, in fact, it encourages just the opposite. It encourages the one surviving newspaper to try to become all things to all people, to dread controversy rather than embrace it."

Ted Rall, one of the most controversial cartoonists in America, blasts the mainstream press for buckling under whenever faced with reader complaints. In 2004, the *New York Times* Web site dropped Rall's syndicated strip after running it for several years. "While nytimes.com and its parent company support the right of free expression," maintained the Web site's editor, Len Apcar, in an interview with the *Progressive*. "We also recognize an obligation to assure our users that what we publish, no matter what its origin, does not offend the reasonable sensibilities of our audience."

But what portion of the audience was offended, and just how reasonable were their sensibilities? The *Times* revealed that it started "monitoring" Rall's work in March 2002, when their Web site posted, then pulled, "Terror Widows," a strip that questioned whether some family members of 9/11 victims might be tantalized by fame and fortune—an unconventional but thought-provoking premise. "It's a send-up of the commodification of grief. It's an absolutely tasteless cartoon, and it needed to be to talk about an absolutely tasteless thing," explained Rall in the *Progressive*. He accuses the *Times* Web site of jettisoning him because they could not be bothered responding to e-mail complaints about his work generated by right-wing bloggers. Though the Internet provides cartoonists with a way to disseminate censored cartoons, it also makes it easy for partisan activists to register protests out of all proportion to their numbers.

Apprehension about reader reaction undoubtedly caused most American newspapers and magazines to limit coverage of the "intoonfadah"—the violent protests that followed the September 2005 publication of twelve cartoons featuring the likeness of Mohammed by the Danish newspaper *Jyllands-Posten*. Though Amir Taheri pointed out in the *Wall Street Journal* that actually "there is no Quranic injunction against images, whether of Muhammad or anyone else," many Moslems consider pictorial representation of the religion's founding prophet blasphemy. Like most American newspapers, the *Boston Globe* and the *Boston Phoenix*—the city's most widely read daily and alternative weekly—wrote about the Danish cartoons but shied away from reprinting any. "Newspapers ought to refrain from publishing offensive caricatures of Mohammed in the name of the ultimate Enlightenment value: tolerance," editorialized the *Globe*, which neglected to acknowledge any concern about vendettas, as the *Phoenix* forthrightly did. Calling it "the darkest moment in our 40-year publishing history," the editors of the *Phoenix* admitted that "fear of retaliation from the international brotherhood of radical and bloodthirsty Islamists" was their primary reason for not running the Mohammed cartoons.

In an interview with *Jyllands-Posten*, as Pulitzer Prize–winning cartoonist Doug Marlette, who has received death threats for his cartoons about Islamic fundamentalists, cautioned that by suppressing the Mohammed cartoons the American media abdicated its responsibility to keep the public informed. In this case, he argued, self-censorship was tantamount to acquiescing to mob rule. "You don't need protection to sell advertising or to confirm popular beliefs. You need protection to express unpopular opinions," said Marlette. "And our ability to engage in vigorous debate and to tolerate robust intellectual discourse and all the attendant controversies is a measure of the health of society."

For more evidence of the don't-rock-the-boat mentality now infecting newsrooms, consider the 2004 decision by clients of Continental Features—a consortium that produces a Sunday comics section for a few dozen newspapers—to cancel *Doonesbury*. In an e-mail to clients that accompanied a survey about *Doonesbury*, the company's president, Van Wilkerson, lobbied against running the award-winning, liberal strip: "I have fielded numerous complaints about *Doonesbury* in the past and feel it is time to drop this feature and add another in its place." The unpopularity contest wasn't even that close: papers voted 21 to 15 to dispatch Zonker, B.D., and crew. As a replacement, Continental's clients opted for *Get Fuzzy*, which chronicles the wacky misadventures of an advertising executive and his pets, Bucky Katt and Satchel Pooch.

Illustrators have struggled lately, too, as magazines increasingly limit artistic freedom, pay stagnant rates, and run more photographs to reduce the risk of publishing incendiary images. "Editors are afraid of illustration, and they've convinced themselves that photography is what sells on the newsstand," says acclaimed designer Walter Bernard in the *New York Review of Magazines*. Illustrator Mirko Ilic, born in Bosnia, finds it ironic that he endures more suppression in the United States than he did in Communist Yugoslavia. "I published there three hundred posters. I published there five hundred different record covers. I did comics. I did thousands and thousands of political illustrations, I never draw one [draft] sketch in my life," says Ilic in his Manhattan studio. "First time I heard the word 'sketch' was when I did my first *Time* magazine cover. I said,

'Why do you need a sketch?' [The art director said,] 'To show the editor.' [I said,] 'But your function is art *director*. I don't get it.' "

Steve Brodner, an editor as well as an artist, suggests that publications often scrub illustrations to kowtow to advertisers: "Before, advertisers wouldn't think to complain that an 'ugly' illustration about a war or something would be next to their ad. Now they do. . . . Even if they had complained twenty or thirty years ago, they may not have been listened to." Writing in the *Columbia Journalism Review*, investigative reporter Russ Baker cited many cases of advertiser chutzpah, including the written demand by Kimberly Clark, the manufacturer of Huggies diapers, that magazines such as *Parenting* and *Sesame Street* position their ads "adjacent to black and white happy baby editorial."

Those who consider journalism to be like any other business—words as widgets—will deem dumping *Doonesbury* or nixing an illustration to mollify a diaper advertiser as reasonable marketing decisions. Find out what clients want and give it to them. The conglomerate that pays the bills is always right. Such narrow thinking, which ignores the constitutionally protected public service component of the profession, may explain why so many cartoonists are now losing their jobs.

Since 1975, about two-thirds of America's independent newspapers have disappeared, meaning that large publicly held chains beholden to Wall Street now dominate much of the print media. As the Associated Press pointed out: "Newspapers owned by publicly held companies earned an average of 20.5 cents on the dollar in 2004, a very healthy margin for any business." That's nearly double what companies in the Standard & Poor's index of large U.S. companies made in 2004.

But stockholders demand *constant* growth, so, despite profit margins that would make manufacturers salivate, the bean counters at newspapers gut editorial staffs—a book section here, a Sunday magazine there, cartoonists everywhere. The inevitable diminution in coverage and quality contributes to the consistent drop in paid newspaper circulation, which, according to the Associated Press, fell 2.6 percent in a six-month period ending in September 2005, more evidence of a "years-long trend."

With nationally syndicated cartoons cheap to purchase, newspapers increasingly consider staff cartoonists expendable. "You face the question: Do you hire an investigative reporter? Do you hire a city council reporter? Do you hire a cartoonist? I can't buy a city council reporter through syndication, I can't buy an investigative reporter through syndication, but I can get the cartoonist," reasoned Bruce Dold, editorial page editor of the *Chicago Tribune*, on National Public Radio in 2005. A few years earlier, Dold, whose paper once employed three cartoonists and now has none, sounded less ambivalent about cartoons. He acknowledged to a reporter at his own paper that cartoons are "the best read thing on the editorial page."

According to cartoonist J. P. Trostle, writing in *Nieman Reports*, the number of staff cartoonists at U.S. newspapers plummeted from nearly two hundred in the early 1980s to less than ninety in 2004. The ranks only get thinner. In late 2005, renowned cartoonist Kevin Kallaugher accepted a buyout from the *Baltimore Sun* "rather than wait for the ax to drop on my position," he told a trade magazine, and the *Los Angeles Times* canned Pulitzer Prize winner Michael Ramirez. Neither paper plans to hire replacements.

The silencing of editorial artists—historically a progressive voice in the press—comes at a time when the mainstream media bends over backward—or just bends over—to appease conservatives. The shift to the right became apparent after Republicans won control of both houses of Congress in 1994. The bootlicking increased when George W. Bush took office in 2001 and intensified after 9/11. Mark Fiore noticed the increasingly repressive atmosphere at the *San Jose Mercury News*. Management urged him to soften cartoons aimed at the Bush administration; rather than comply with that dictate, Fiore left the paper. Illustrator Anita Kunz says she enjoyed carte blanche to skewer the first President Bush but now must exercise more caution when portraying the second. "Despite the fact that everybody says 'liberal media, liberal media,' I don't find it that way at all," she says. Peter Kuper, an illustrator and comic artist, describes the post-9/11 period as "an extremely touchy time . . . when everybody was terrified to say anything that didn't line up behind the president." Paul Szep, formerly the political cartoonist at the *Boston Globe*, agrees. "Cartoonists can't do anything," he laments, contrasting recent years with the Vietnam era, when he made his name. "I've given up on the heavy-duty stuff. I can't get things printed on a regular basis."

Since 9/11 some liberal editorial artists have lost their jobs because of their politics; others tell me they expect pink slips so they now pull their punches. Shortly after I started hunting for contributions for this book, a cartoonist working at a weekly newspaper in a red state got in touch with me. The artist, who was excited about the prospect of having work in this book, complained that the weekly paper's publisher frequently killed cartoons opposing the war in Iraq. I expected a batch of killed cartoons to choose from, but instead I received this letter of regret:

> Thank you so very, very kindly for your invitation to mail you some radical killed cartoons. I regret to tell you that I'd probably better not. I've been talking with my editors (past and present) to be certain of my submission to you—there were some 30 cartoons on the anti-war subject that have been killed most viciously. BUT the editors tell me—as do several others who know the publisher—that I'm barely hanging on by a thread there as it is due to my "radicalness." To be included in such a book as you propose would spell certain death to my career as a cartoonist here. . . . While on the one

hand I feel like I'm chickening out, I want to "live to fight another day" so to speak.

Editors do not work in a vacuum. The rise in media self-censorship coincides with the Bush administration's overt hostility toward the press. President Bush might bestow chummy nicknames on journalists—he calls Candy Crowley of CNN "Dulce" (Spanish for "candy")—but his actions communicate obvious disdain for most reporters. In 2004, the Bush administration banned correspondents for the *New York Times* from traveling on Dick Cheney's airplane, because the paper reported extensively about the vice president's ties to his former employer, Halliburton. The Bushies punished aggressive *Washington Post* White House correspondent Dana Milbank by cutting off his access to official sources. Bush's Justice Department is investigating *New York Times* reporters Eric Lichtblau and James Risen, who broke the story of the president's illicit domestic spying program—a revelation that some Bush boosters equate to "treason." Meanwhile, the Federal Emergency Management Agency blocked reporters from boats rescuing the victims of Hurricane Katrina, preventing the public from seeing the disastrous results of the federal government's bungled response to the storm. The Defense Department also gets the picture. They prohibited the press from taking photos of the coffins of soldiers killed in combat and revoked the press passes of two embedded journalists who photographed Humvees damaged by Iraqi insurgents.

Even the Secret Service plays the intimidation game. In 2003, the *Los Angeles Times* turned away a Secret Service agent who tried to question Michael Ramirez, then the paper's cartoonist, though he had drawn a pro-Bush cartoon. The drawing in question featured a gunman with the word "Politics" on his back pointing a gun at the head of the president. The background is labeled "Iraq." Ramirez borrowed from the iconic image of a South Vietnamese general executing a Communist prisoner at point-blank range; he hoped to suggest that the president was a victim of "political assassination" by critics who argued that he exaggerated the threat posed by Saddam Hussein.

Most recently, official contempt for the free press was plain to see when U.S. State Department spokesman Sean McCormack denigrated the Danish cartoons of Mohammed—protected speech by artists who have been forced into hiding because of death threats from the likes of Osama bin Laden—as "anti-Muslim" and "unacceptable." Yet it's increasingly clear that what is truly unacceptable is the coordinated attack by the White House on a profession enshrined in the Constitution.

A dolf Hitler understood the power of cartoonists. The Nazi propaganda sheet *Der Stürmer* ran many hateful caricatures of Jews. But cartoonists who opposed the Nazis were denounced as "degenerate artists" and "supreme enemies of the State." On May 27, 1944, the Nazis executed several Polish cartoonists for drawing anti-Fascist images. Given the opportunity, Hitler would doubtless have arranged the same fate for British cartoonist David Low, who forewarned the West about the dangers of the Nazis. The Gestapo put Low on a hit list. Stalin also appreciated the influence of cartoonists; he once summoned Russian cartoonist Boris Efimov to his office, where he critiqued a caricature of Dwight Eisenhower and recommended changes. Talk about a scary editor.

"Dictators of the right and the left fear the political cartoonist more than they do the atomic bomb. No totalitarian government can afford to be ridiculed," humorist Art Buchwald once said. Indeed, when despots rule, cartoonists die. During the "Dirty War" in Argentina, Hector Oesterheld, who often portrayed leaders of the military junta controlling the country as aliens, disappeared in 1976 along with his four daughters.

In 1995, Algerian cartoonist Brahim Guerroui was kidnapped and murdered. Rebels in Sierra Leone killed Muniru Turay, one of the country's leading cartoonists, in 1999, then burned down the office of his newspaper. Incidents of cartoonists being jailed, assaulted, and exiled are too numerous to mention.

Unlike their colleagues in the developing world, editorial artists in North America don't face assassination, beatings, or dank jail cells, but they have received unwelcome attention from American politicians with totalitarian tendencies. Richard Nixon placed *Los Angeles Times* cartoonist Paul Conrad on his "enemies list," and J. Edgar Hoover closely monitored *Mad* magazine and kept a file on publisher William M. Gaines. The longtime director of the FBI also proposed commissioning cartoons to disrupt "the New Left." In a July 5, 1968, memo to an underling, Hoover posited: "Consider the use of cartoons . . . which will have the effect of ridiculing the New Left. Ridicule is one of the most potent weapons which we can use."

When free to deploy the potent weapon of ridicule by courageous editors, cartoonists, illustrators, and comic artists have enriched America. At their best, editorial art reaches out from the static pages of newspapers and magazines, and now the Web, and pokes readers in the eyes. They sting us in a primitive place, forcing us to question our leaders, our neighbors, our values.

During the start of the cold war, long before Edward R. Murrow confronted Joseph McCarthy on live television, *Washington Post* cartoonist Herbert Block bravely stood up to the senator from Wisconsin and his Red-baiting goon squad. Block, who coined the term "McCarthyism," consistently spanked McCarthy and his allies in print at the height of their power—a time when many progressive artists, including cartoonists, were losing their careers. Block was almost, but not entirely, alone in his battle with McCarthy. In May 1953, *Pogo* creator Walt Kelly introduced a character named Simple J. Malarkey, a snarling bobcat with a resemblance to the scheming senator. Afraid to rile McCarthy, some newspapers would not run the strip whenever Malarkey made a cameo in the Okefenokee Swamp. "By laughing at McCarthy," *Washington Post* book critic Jonathan Yardley observed, "Kelly almost certainly played a significant role in that demagogue's eventual disgrace."

In the early 1960s, Norman Rockwell did not get a nightstick to the ribs while marching from Selma to Montgomery, but his illustrations depicting scenes of racism in *Look* magazine shocked many cosseted Americans and at least alerted them to the civil rights movement. Then there was David Levine's 1966 caricature of Lyndon Johnson showing off a scar on his stomach shaped like a map of Vietnam (an allusion to a press conference in which LBJ flashed reporters in an attempt to silence rumors that he was seriously ill after a gall bladder operation). "No photograph damaged Lyndon Johnson so much as David Levine's waspish drawing of L.B.J. lifting his shirt," concluded *Time* magazine. Without question, brutal combat on TV galvanized the American public against the Vietnam War, but cartoonists, including Levine, Edward Sorel, Paul Szep, and Paul Conrad raised alarms as well. "Their passionate, pointed commentary combined with televised images of death and destruction to discourage LBJ from running for reelection and, ultimately, bring an end to the war," wrote cartoon historian Harry Katz in *Nieman Reports*.

We may look back and credit the cartoons of Ted Rall, Clay Bennett, and Mike Luckovich, among others, with helping to drive public opinion against the Iraq War. Luckovich was awarded the 2005 Pulitzer Prize for one of the most memorable images in recent years—writing out the names of 2,000 soldiers killed in Iraq to form the word "WHY?" Cartoonists—at least for the time being—still matter.

INTRODUCTION

As Stephen Hess and Sandy Northrop noted in their 1996 book, *Drawn & Quartered: The History of American Political Cartoons*, "The political cartoon is the embodiment of the American form of government. Democracy is fed by encouraging a free forum for discussion." But that forum, as you are about to see, is not nearly as free as it once was or should be.

EDITOR'S NOTE

The cartoons, comics, and illustrations that follow were submitted to newspapers and magazines by artists who were either on staff, regular contributors, or freelancers on assignment. The drawings were then rejected. Many of the drawings are previously unpublished; some were published on Web sites or ultimately found homes in other publications. Most artists have presented their work as they submitted it to editors. Peter Kuper, Patrick O'Connor, and Matt Davies chose to ink nearly completed sketches.

Harry Katz, curator of the Herb Block Foundation Collection, wrote the text accompanying Block's cartoon on pages 121–22. Ernest Dumas wrote the essay accompanying his longtime colleague George Fisher's cartoon on pages 124–25. All other précis are written by David Wallis, who interviewed most of the book's contributors. Alex Rawls conducted interviews with Derf, Josh Eiserike, Rainer Hachfeld, Steve Kelley, Keith Knight, Peter Kuper, Carol Lay, and Pete Wagner. Admittedly, the artists' accounts of the killings are subjective in nature.

I

INDECENT EXPOSURE

FROM SEX TO DEATH

CHAMPIONS OF BREAKFAST

Success to Paul Conrad means ruining your appetite. The three-time Pulitzer Prize winner—famous for cartoons so scathing that Richard Nixon placed him on an enemies list—sometimes fails what many editors refer to as the "breakfast test": *When you open the newspaper in the morning and see a cartoon, do eggs over easy suddenly go down hard?*

Conrad, who consciously simplified his drawing style over the years so as not to obscure the cartoon's point with elaborate art, unabashedly uses nudity and sexual imagery if it helps him bolster an argument. He drew Nixon's press-hating vice president, Spiro Agnew, pissing on newspapers. Another cartoon showed Saddam Hussein exposing his bare ass to the world, symbolizing the dictator's contempt for the international community. Neither cartoon made it past editors at the *Los Angeles Times*.

David Levine's controversial illustration of Henry Kissinger raping the world (which led feminist staffers at the *Nation* to protest the portrayal of the world as a woman) clearly influenced Conrad. "I thought Levine's was absolutely one of the best cartoons I had ever seen—until I saw mine," Conrad says, referring to his drawing of an aggressive elephant mounting a startled donkey. His editor called it "thigh-slapping fun" in an interview with a local alternative weekly but spiked it anyway. Conrad conjured up the cartoon to denounce Republicans who were bellowing about bipartisanship while pushing for Bill Clinton's impeachment. "When the Democrats controlled the House, those were good days," says Conrad. "Check some of those bills. You will find a bipartisan Congress who got the job done."

In a bid to slip the sex scene past his paper's decency patrol, Conrad omitted any hint of genitalia from the drawing and concentrated on the faces of the donkey and elephant. "I thought the expression on the elephant's face was sheer joy," roars Conrad. "The poor donkey doesn't know what hit him."

PAUL CONRAD

Killed by the Los Angeles Times, 1999

CONGRESSIONAL BIPARTISANSHIP

COVERING UP

Asked why his former editor at the *San Diego Union-Tribune* killed his cartoon about the skimpy clothes kids wear today, Steve Kelley redraws the image in a notebook and points to a smidgen of exposed butt crack. "That right there," he whoops over lunch at Dino's Bar & Grill, a po-boy place in New Orleans. Kelley now works at the *Times-Picayune* in New Orleans because he was fired by the *Union-Tribune* after the butt crack brouhaha of 2001.

"My editor at the time—who's very priggish, very fastidious—he got all 'Oh, you can't show a butt crack.' I said the cartoon really doesn't work without it, and if you go to the shopping center across the street, you'll see *a thousand butt cracks*. They show butt cracks on TV all the time. It's like cleavage."

Kelley says he offered to shorten the vertical line of the butt crack, and the editorial page editor—a man Kelley says disapproved of lingerie ads in the paper—agreed to have another look. The following day, Kelley brought in a revised version of the cartoon, but his editor and the paper's senior editor were not in their offices. Kelley left the cartoon with a third editor charged with layout, a decision he considered within standard operating procedure. Kelley says the paper's senior editor later pulled the butt crack cartoon and accused him of "trying to sneak" it into print. Kelley responded with colorful language, and was soon out of a job.

He believes that his editor was looking for an excuse to oust him. "He didn't like me, he didn't like my work, he didn't like it politically, he didn't like that I made more money than him, and he decided to make a big deal over it." Regardless, the fact that such a mild cartoon sparked such a wild battle speaks volumes about the prudish nature of many newspapers.

"The reality of creating comics for papers in the USA is you avoid or treat with kid gloves topics such as sex," says Carol Lay, whose witty treatment of anal sex (page 34) was ushered out the *San Francisco Examiner's* back door. Lay says the *Examiner's* editor loved the cartoon, but the paper's publisher "thought it inappropriate for children."

More often than not, "protecting the children" is the pretext for puritanism, but is the print media really protecting children by clinging to Nelson conventions in a Soprano culture? Recent studies by more than one state found increases in the number of cases of chlamydia, gonorrhea, HIV, and syphilis. And, according to sex therapist Dr. Sylvia Hacker, professor emerita at the University of Michigan, sex-positive countries such as the Netherlands have, per capita, about one-eighth as many teenage pregnancies and sexually transmitted diseases as does the United States. (Dr. Hacker, known as "the Dr. Ruth of the Midwest," did not last long before the *Detroit Free Press* dropped her frank advice column Let's Talk About Sex.)

The federal government, which now promotes abstinence as a public health policy, and schools deserve more blame than the media for contributing to the spread of sexually transmitted diseases. But the press is at least partly culpable for fostering negative attitudes about sex. Remember former surgeon general Dr. Jocelyn Elders? In 1994, President Bill Clinton discarded her like a used condom for musing that sex education curriculum "perhaps" should include information about masturbation. "One Gaffe Too Many," declared the *New York Times*. Elders "crossed the line between outspokenness and political self-destruction," opined the *Bangor Daily News*. And the editorial page editor of the *Kansas City Star* diagnosed Elders with "unstoppable diarrhea of the mouth." The *Star* also demurred when Lee Judge submitted a cartoon about Elders's unceremonious firing (page 35).

In 2001, when Elders's successor as surgeon general, Dr. David Satcher, advocated a broad range of sex education (minus the masturbation lessons), George W. Bush's first press secretary, Ari Fleischer, dismissed the initiative, saying, "The president understands the report was issued by a Surgeon General that he did not appoint." Satcher's report, unsurprisingly, was barely covered in the media.

STEVE KELLEY

Killed by the *San Diego Union-Tribune*, 2001

CAROL LAY

Killed by the *San Francisco Examiner*, undated

LEE JUDGE

Killed by the *Kansas City Star*, 1994

Q. WHY DID PRESIDENT CLINTON GET RID OF JOYCELYN ELDERS?

A. SHE RUBBED HIM THE WRONG WAY.

SHOTGUN MARRIAGE: ESQUIRE & WAL-MART

"**E**very month I'm hired to do a drawing about sex, but I'm not allowed to draw people *having* sex," chuckles John Cuneo, who illustrates an advice column for *Esquire* about the erotic arts. Men's magazines are the teases of publishing. They allow illustrators more freedom to titillate than newspapers allow editorial cartoonists, but when artists come up with penetrating ideas . . . *um, shouldn't you take a cold shower?*

There are explanations for limits on explicit imagery. National advertisers may look the other way when photo spreads of starlets in string bikinis pop off the pages of men's magazines, but actual nudity is usually a no-no. Publications such as *Esquire*, *GQ*, and *Maxim* try to be sexy enough to snag male readers, but not as sexually graphic as *Playboy* and *Penthouse*, which might turn off mainstream advertisers. "Nobody wants to be the media buyer who buys an ad that blows up in his client's face," says Keith Kelly, the *New York Post*'s media columnist. Kelly adds that magazines worry about offending retailers, who have been known to hide issues behind counters if they regard photos or illustrations as too risqué. Wal-Mart, which sells about 15 percent of all magazines on newsstands in America, banned *Maxim* and other "lad mags" in 2003, and has wrapped the bare shoulders of *Vogue*, *Cosmo*, and *Redbook* with the equivalents of plastic shawls to protect shoppers from cover chatter about the best orgasms ever.

A few years back, Cuneo thought that magazines were loosening up. *Esquire* offered him space for a column with no stated parameters—an illustrator's dream. Damn Good Advice, which Cuneo describes as "free-association cartoons," delivered big-brotherly lessons on everything from grooming to can't-miss pickup lines. But *Esquire* turned down most of Cuneo's erotic sketches, such as his "dirty little drawing" that redefined the pizza party.

Given the confines of magazine illustration, Cuneo has learned to celebrate little victories. "I broke through the nipple barrier this year," he boasts. "They are *humorous* nipples. They are not photographic nipples. Normally, *Esquire* doesn't want to go into the realm of anything too specific anatomically. Next year, I'm hoping for pubic hair."

JOHN CUNEO

Killed by *Esquire*, 2004

DAMN GOOD ADVICE

NOTHING BEATS A ROMANTIC DINNER AT HOME.

WE HAVE MET THE ENEMY AND HE IS US

Keith Knight's editor at the *San Francisco Examiner* visibly squirmed as she read the first four panels of his strip about a trigger-happy dad who "bonds" with his son by producing a gun from his pants. Her face "bent out of shape," recalls Knight, until she reached the fifth panel and sighed in relief. The bulge in the father's pants proved to be a pistol.

Nevertheless, the editor shot down the strip. She offered no explanation of her decision, though Knight assumes that the mere allusion to sexual abuse made her uncomfortable. Three weeks later, he did a takeoff on the X Games, called *The V Games*—V standing for Viagra. "It was all about old men's penises. Instead of the pole vault—well, it was the *pole vault*—with guys' penises. And fencing with guys' penises." That one ran without a fuss.

The randomness of rejection still mystifies Knight. "It's your job as the artist to create, and it's so random what they think is offensive that if you play the editor, you'll drive yourself crazy." That said, as he reflects on his career, one trend emerges: editors in supposedly liberal bastions such as San Francisco clamp down on his comics far more than editors in seemingly conservative cities. "I always say, 'Look, this is running in *Salt Lake City.*' "

Knight suspects that more cautious editors tend to disingenuously adopt the perceived sensitivities of their readers. "I drew a drawing of me with a big boulder of crack, and I was standing in an alley with crack hookers around me saying, '*Ooh, lookee here.* A bunch of crack and no one to smoke it with,' " he says. His editor at a northern California alternative weekly rejected the cartoon, and Knight, who is African American, remembers the debate about race that ensued:

> Editor: "We don't want our readers to think that *we* think all black people smoke crack."
> Knight: "What are you talking about? Does it say that in your editorial?"
> Editor: "No, but it says that in your comic strip."
> Knight: "No, it says *I* smoke crack."
> Editor: "What's the point?"
> Knight: "No point. It's just funny."
> Editor: "We have a large white liberal readership and we do not want to offend them."

"She thought I was offending white people, which was the strangest thing I've heard anybody say to me."

KEITH KNIGHT

Killed by the *San Francisco Examiner*, undated

NOT USING YOUR HEAD

In the movie *The Paper*, set in a New York City tabloid newsroom, top editor Henry Hackett (Michael Keaton) berates his art department about a shoddy illustration accompanying a story about penile implants: "Could we possibly get a better dick drawing? This one looks like a map of Florida."

The Paper won raves for its realistic portrayal of daily journalism, but a newsroom debate over proper penis art? Doubtful. With the exception of the John Wayne Bobbitt penipalooza, male frontal nudity ranks among the American media's most untouchable taboos. Mike Keefe's cartoon of Uncle Sam (page 44) with a flaccid Florida-shaped penis did not make the cut at the *Denver Post*. "About that time, two things were going on," recalls Keefe. "There was the debacle of the [2000] election results, and Bob Dole was doing erectile dysfunction commercials on television." Keefe says he knew his cartoon would never run, but he did it anyway, like a teenager testing his parents' boundaries. "If you never cross the line," says Keefe, "you are reluctant to approach the line.

"We're an odd mix of a puritanical society and a sex-crazed society at the same time," he continues. "There's a strong Christian fundamentalist element to our society that helps dictate values from one end, and then there's Hollywood and liberal-minded people that dictate culture from the other end."

Milt Priggee, whose sexually inquisitive but fully clothed Uncle Sam (page 45) was scrapped by the *Spokesman-Review* in Spokane, Washington, agrees with Keefe. "People say America is Victorian in its attitudes toward sex. The public ain't nothing compared to a newspaper," says Priggee. His cartoon was inspired by news about a sex survey that found Europeans made love more often than Americans did. "I think I had a safe cartoon. It's not about Ronald Reagan. I don't [target] advertisers here. No one has a hard-on. No underwear is showing. No cleavage. Nothing. The editor said, 'You drew Uncle Sam's *thing.*' "

In the analysis of David Friedman, author of *A Mind of Its Own: A Cultural History of the Penis* and a former newspaper reporter, the editors who killed the ribald Uncle Sams had more on their minds than safeguarding readers from impropriety. "The idea that a nation's power and virility is embodied sexually is at least as old as the Romans. Roman generals sometimes promoted soldiers based on penis size. Perhaps the bowtie-wearing editorial-page editor unconsciously realized that for Uncle Sam to look down and see a limp penis offended his sense that America was a powerful, virile, manly nation."

MIKE KEEFE

Killed by the Denver Post, *2000*

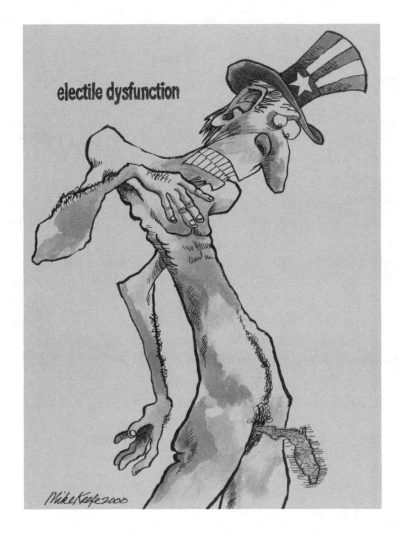

MILT PRIGGEE

Killed by the *Spokesman-Review*, 1998

SLICK'S WILLY

As part of his strategy to ward off meddling from editors at the *Montreal Gazette,* Terry Mosher (Aislin) struck a deal with a local radio station. He faxes rejected cartoons to the DJs. "At six o'clock in the morning, during drive-time, they would say, 'By the way, we have a cartoon that the *Gazette* wouldn't run yesterday,'" says Mosher. "The editors got to know that, and that makes them nervous to kill a cartoon."

Though he's mellowed with age, Mosher also uses purposeful gruffness to distance editors. "Editors by nature are going to step on you. They can't help themselves." He also worries that aggressive editing thwarts cartoonists from doing their duty, which he defines as "pointing out that the king is syphilitic and has a mistress." So when the *Montreal Gazette's* publisher requested that Mosher draw a flattering caricature to present to Bill Clinton, who would be in town attending a fund-raiser, Mosher's response—"No, no, fuck that. I'm not going to do it"—surprised no one.

"But I went home," Mosher recalls, "and my wife said, 'He's raising a million bucks for a children's hospital. Stop being such a goddamned prima donna. It's a million bucks, for God's sakes. Be nice for once in your life.' "

That was not easy for Mosher; he drew Clinton with a protruding saxophone penis, and the publisher passed on it. *Children's hospital. Must remember children's hospital.* Mosher's encore featured Clinton playing sax, pants zipped, jamming. It hangs in the former president's Harlem office and appeared on the front page of the *Gazette.*

Clinton reminds Mosher of "the guys I used to drink with—confident guys I used to drink with . . . He has a very expressive face. [George W.] Bush is easy, and easy guys you don't enjoy that much. Bush has one or two expressions, but Clinton has a 'Hi there, how are you doing,' glad-handing personality."

Mosher argues that many cartoonists today, especially Americans, share Clinton's desire to be universally liked. "Syndication has helped to kill cartooning in the United States," Mosher complains. "[Cartoonists] don't want to upset a housewife in Albuquerque, so they take it easy, and they want the housewife in Albuquerque to understand the cartoon, so they deal [with] . . . the news out of Washington, Viagra jokes. It's a big problem, because it is all generic. In Canada, we might make a few bucks out of syndication, but it's not a big deal. . . . When I do a cartoon of the mayor, he sees it. It has a lot more impact."

Mosher counsels cartoonists to return to their roots. "We came out of fly sheets on the street. That's where [cartooning] started in England and in France—little publications that criticized the local establishment. . . . For cartooning to survive, we have to go back to going after local figures and stop this McTooning that satisfies everyone."

TERRY MOSHER (AISLIN)

Killed by the *Montreal Gazette*, 2002

MAN ON A MISSION

"**F**amily newspapers are family newspapers," says Clay Bennett, sounding a bit cautious. Bennett was explaining why he did not object when the *St. Petersburg Times* spiked his suggestive, but in no way obscene, send-up of Bill Clinton's sexual escapades (page 51).

Whipping the president for his illicit affairs was fair game to Bennett, given that the details of Paula Jones's sexual harassment lawsuit against Clinton were widely reported. "Her charges seemed in character with Clinton's—you know—psychosis," says Bennett.

Bennett defers to editors on matters of taste, saving protests for quests to suppress his politics. He bitterly recalls how the *St. Petersburg Times* silenced him during the first Gulf War. "I was allowed to rail on . . . until the bullets started flying, and then the boot heel of conventional thinking came down on me with a thud."

At the *Christian Science Monitor*, where Bennett has worked since 1997, he embraces the newspaper's motto: "To injure no man, but to bless all mankind." He has more freedom than ever to tackle tough political issues—criticizing the Iraq War despite the boots on the ground, for instance—but he avoids personal attacks. "Many years ago when I was full of spunk and vinegar—which I still am full of—I would go after Reagan and the Reagan administration tooth and claw. The whole point for me was to make them look as bad as possible, to make my comments as strongly as possible and to slap my readers right across the face every single day." Now Bennett sees his mission as "bringing people into your church—not just preaching to the ones that are already there." He continues: "If you use your brain a little bit more and use your tact a little bit better, you can still make strong points without calling people names."

CLAY BENNETT

Killed by the *St. Petersburg Times*, 1994

SHITTY BUSINESS

The cartoons that Matt Davies grew up with in England overflowed with piss and shit. Plenty of fart jokes as well. "The biggest, biggest difference between U.S. and UK cartoonists is scatological references," says Davies, who seems a tad jealous of his British colleagues' ability to get poop published. "Steve Bell [of the *Guardian*] did a cartoon. The title was something like The UN's Role in Iraq. It was a toilet paper roll with the UN logo on it. He had [George W.] Bush sitting on a toilet and there was just shit all over the place. His editors were like, '*Whoa*, this is a lot of shit.'" Bell later deleted "two or three turds," says Davies, whose editors at the *Journal News*, in White Plains, New York, would not even consider running such a cartoon. Davies can include toilet bowls, and once plopped a mound of elephant dung in a cartoon to represent Republican excess, but his newspaper generally bars excrement. Editors deemed Davies's cartoon about Bush's disregard for America's traditional allies during the Iraq adventure as excessive.

Newspapers, predicts Davies, will relax their standards as the business expands online. "[Newspapers] are savvy that their competition is on the Internet, and on the Internet you can find *anything*. But that said, a lot of readers are the older generation who are still kind of squeamish. I don't understand it, but I respect it."

Despite his appreciation of toilet humor, Davies, surprisingly, hopes he would resist the temptation of a fecal-friendly policy. "The problem with scatological cartoons is if you are allowed to use them, you kind of stop thinking. You just go, 'OK, George Bush is a pile of turds.' And you are done thinking. . . . The role of a cartoonist is to go way further than that. It behooves an editorial cartoonist to put certain images off-limits—not to self-censor but, on the contrary, to inspire creativity."

MATT DAVIES

Killed by the *Journal News*, 2004

CURSED CARTOONS

In his essay entitled "Are We On the Edge?" cartoonist and historian R. C. Harvey reveals how newspapers and syndicates in the 1930s enforced stifling standards on comic strip artists, drastically restricting the words they could use in print: "No swear words ever appeared; no deity's name was ever taken in vain. . . . [R]eferences to drinking and drunkenness—or mention of liquor or beer—were prohibited. . . . And there could be no references to diseases, infirmities, operations, or other such 'morbid' subjects. Way into the 1950s, some syndicates forbade cartoonists to depict snakes in their strips."

Today's cartoonists have a racier vocabulary to work with (snakes now pass muster too). Still, publishers continue to place limits on the language that cartoonists can use, sometimes stubbornly so. At a 1984 campaign rally on the docks of New Jersey, then–Vice President George H. W. Bush was picked up by an open mike boasting that he "kicked a little ass" the night before in his debate against Democrat VP hopeful Geraldine Ferraro. The scripted, unscripted moment motivated Lee Judge of the *Kansas*

City Star to draw a cartoon (opposite), but quoting the word "ass" doomed the drawing.

More recently, in a climate where the House voted to raise fines on potty-mouthed broadcasters and entertainers who flout "decency" standards from $32,500 to $500,000 per violation, several newspapers declined to run a 2005 *Doonesbury* strip that included a reference to Karl Rove as "Turd Blossom." Considering that it had been widely reported that President Bush gave his senior advisor the scatological nickname, the decision seems unduly cautious.

Curses need not be spelled out to rankle editors. The German newspaper *Neues Deutschland* scrubbed Rainer Hachfeld's cartoon (page 58) about the unpopular nominations of John R. Bolton as U.S. ambassador to the United Nations and Paul Wolfowitz to head the World Bank because Bush's combative avatar gives the world the so-called *"stinke-finger."* Again, cartoonists are held to stricter standards than photographers or writers. In 1976, Vice President Nelson Rockefeller famously flipped the bird at hecklers. The *Arkansas Gazette*, like many newspapers, put a photo of Rockefeller gesturing on page one, but it resisted running George Fisher's cartoon close-up of the vice president's extending middle finger.

So called "family newspapers" aren't the only ones to G-rate their pages. The *Nation* passed up the chance to run Edward Sorel's wonderfully profane cartoon about profanity (page 59). "There's a part of me offended by fuck, fuck, fuck, in movies. I grew up when married couples couldn't be [portrayed] in the same bed," explains Sorel, who accepted his longtime editor Victor Navasky's decision to kill the cartoon. Sorel usually received unfettered freedom from Navasky—"a First Amendment zealot"—and he understands his editor's rationale. "Most of the *Nation's* subscribers are also members of AARP," Sorel chortled, "so fuck still has shock value."

Maybe so. But artists such as Sorel, Hachfeld, and Judge deserve latitude; they curse with purpose.

LEE JUDGE

Killed by the *Kansas City Star*, 1984

RAINER HACHFELD

Killed by *Neues Deutschland,* 2005

EDWARD SOREL

Killed by the *Nation*, undated

NO THANKS FOR THE MEMORIES

The artist known as Derf rejects the suggestion that Bush's Inner Circle was rejected by the *Times of Acadiana* for its anatomical incorrectness: a daisy chain of male asses with heads rammed up them. Rather, he believes that editors at the nominally alternative weekly in Lafayette, Louisiana—once an independently owned paper that's now part of the Gannett empire—hoped to quiet "shrill bawling" from chronically exasperated Bush supporters. "Lafayette couldn't be more red-state. I doubt I would've gotten the same reaction there had it been Michael Moore's Inner Circle."

Derf remembers receiving a white-flag e-mail from the paper's editor. "She was tired of dealing with complaints about these damn cartoons, especially mine . . . and she had decided to just drop *all* the cartoons."

Comic strips are increasingly seen as superfluous by weekly papers, says Derf. He remembers the mid-1980s when strips such as Matt Groening's *Life in Hell,* Lynda Barry's *Ernie Pook's Comeek*, and Bill Griffith's *Zippy the Pinhead* were major attractions in burgeoning alternative weeklies. "Since the [rest of the] content wasn't very good at that point," Derf continues, "people picked up these rags only for the club listings, the personals, and the comics. . . . As the weeklies blossomed and multiplied, so did the comics. In the late eighties, guys like me and Tom Tomorrow and Max Cannon and Ruben Bolling all came on the scene and all had success."

Derf traces the change in the valuation of comics to the late 1990s, when one critical revenue stream began drying up: "Weeklies started cutting back on comics as they lost personals and classifieds to the Internet. When the [ads] went bye-bye, the comics didn't move to the front of the paper; they just got dumped."

Despite the comics' role in defining the alternative weekly's aesthetic, most papers now run just a few strips—"Some not even that," Derf complains. "The odd thing is that comics are *such* cheap content. [Pay] rates have not gone up at all in the past ten years. In fact, I'd say they've fallen. Why? I'm not sure. Editors are word people. Their loyalty lies with their own kind. . . . Many editors opt to run some crappy CD review by some local hack rather than a great comic. We can't help but feel betrayed."

DERF

Killed by the *Times of Acadiana*, 2002

NO RUSH

When a master caricaturist such as Steve Brodner draws a face, he usually resists the obvious: making a big nose bigger or a goofy smile goofier. Instead, he mines the persona to "reveal something . . . that burns itself into a person's brains that they'll never forget."

As a model, Rush Limbaugh offers plenty to exaggerate—a doughy figure, thick eyebrows, a pronounced chin, and a gaping mouth. But Brodner, aside from including Limbaugh's receding hairline and appendage-like cigar in a portrait commissioned and rejected by *Mother Jones*, strategically ignored his other features.

Brodner ass-faces Limbaugh in part because he appreciates the man's talents. "[Limbaugh] is a magnificent entertainer. With a magnificent voice. Quick mind. He's using it to hurt people. Really hurt people. Innocent people," says Brodner. "Anybody in public life who blames victims and tries to turn public opinion against victims is a low-life scumbag."

STEVE BRODNER

Killed by *Mother Jones*, 1993

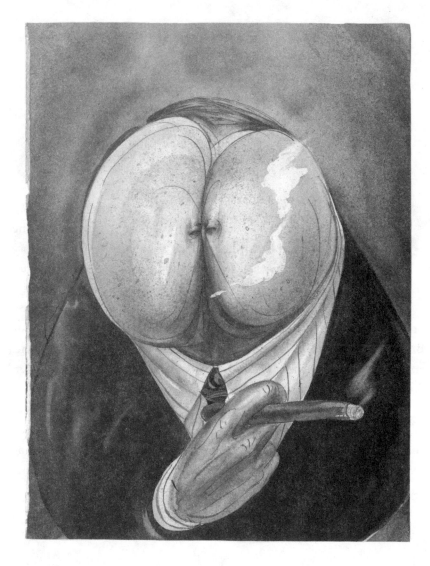

KILL & GRACE

"**T**he most innocuous cartoons get editors riled up," says a puzzled Steve Greenberg, reflecting on his ill-fated memorial cartoon marking the twentieth anniversary of the discovery of AIDS. Greenberg thinks his cartoon merited publication for several reasons: the paper he worked for at the time, the *Marin Independent Journal*, serves many gay readers; a major milestone in the news cried out for commentary; and the cartoon's tone was respectfully somber. "It seemed like a good opportunity to let people know that AIDS is still out there and to note the extent of the disease."

Much to Greenberg's surprise, his editor objected to his AIDS Quilt cartoon (page 67). "She thought it was insensitive to do *any* kind of a cartoon commentary on a subject as tragic as AIDS. It was assuming that cartoons by their very nature had to be humorous. She had a knee-jerk prejudice against cartoons."

Different prejudices can confront cartoonists who tackle issues such as same-sex marriage, gays in the military, and even hate crimes. An editor at the *Scranton Times-Tribune* spiked Dennis Draughon's tribute to Matthew Shepard (page 68), a Wyoming college student who was tortured and beaten to death because of his sexual orientation. According to Chris Lamb's book *Drawn to Extremes: The Use and Abuse of Editorial Cartoons in the United States*, Draughon's editor was just "uncomfortable comparing Shepard with Christ."

Draughon, whose Shepard cartoon won a Golden Spike award (for best killed cartoon) from the Association of American Editorial Cartoonists, suggests that plenty of newspaper editors, as well as too many of his colleagues—largely a fraternity of straight white men—promote homophobia. "Most so-called family newspapers approach homosexuality from a mocking standpoint. Easy jokes. That seems to be the case [with] cartoons I've seen about *Brokeback Mountain*. John Wayne in heaven gets sick in front of a television. They weren't well thought out, but I'm sure they went over well with editors."

STEVE GREENBERG

Killed by the *Marin Independent Journal*, 2001

DENNIS DRAUGHON

Killed by the *Scranton Times-Tribune*, 1998

Father, forgive them; for they know not what they do...

Luke 23:34

DEAD ON ARRIVAL

To hide the government's disastrous response to Hurricane Katrina, the Federal Emergency Management Agency (FEMA) barred news organizations from entering boats recovering the bodies of victims. The bungling agency needn't have resorted to official censorship. The mainstream media typically shies away from publishing or televising corpses, whether on Iraqi battlefields or bobbing in the fetid floodwaters of New Orleans.

The press's discomfort with death extends to cartoons. The *Hartford Courant* passed on Bob Englehart's obituary cartoon of popcorn mogul Orville Redenbacher. "When editors kill a cartoon, it's because they don't feel like they can defend it," says Englehart. "Sometimes if I can give the editor the words to say to the [reader] that calls him on the phone or the politician or the Redenbacher family, then he'll let me go ahead and draw the cartoon."

Englehart acknowledges that obituary cartoons are risky, but "you've got to joke about the things that scare you, right?" His own losses fuel his morbid humor. "You almost need a personal involvement to know what's funny. I lost my mother. My father is getting old. I've lost my father-in-law. I'm well acquainted with death. My mother died of breast cancer. I could do breast cancer cartoons if I wanted to. I know where to stop because I'm personally involved."

Joel Pett's personal experience with the holiday blues inspires his annual cartoon about Christmastime depression. "It's not my favorite time of year. The days are shorter, and you are not getting much light, and the hypocrisy of Christmas is hard to deal with." But Pett's editor got squeamish when he portrayed a suicide in Santa's workshop.

Pett's cartoons usually run, so he requested a postmortem from his editor. "She said, 'When I worked at another paper, some friend of mine had a friend of theirs kill themselves around Christmas. This is a very real thing, and I just couldn't stop thinking about the people in our reader-ship who maybe have had a family member killed around the holidays.'"

Pett replied: "Do you think . . . they're going to have a great Christmas unless they see this [cartoon] and they'll say 'Dad blew his brains out last Christmas, I forgot?'

"If you apply that standard, you can [always] talk yourself out of run-ning one of my cartoons."

BOB ENGLEHART

Killed by the *Hartford Courant*, 1995

" HE KEEPS POPPING OUT OF THE CASKET."

JOEL PETT

Killed by the *Lexington Herald Leader*, undated

KILLING MEANS NEVER
HAVING TO SAY
YOU'RE SORRY

Clayton Hanmer, known as CTON, has no regrets for drawing "a guy talking out of his ass" for Canada's *Globe & Mail* story about empty apologies.

"I'm from a small town outside [Toronto], and when you say you're sorry, you mean it," says Hanmer. "If you don't, then you're going to see that person the next day . . . But when you move to the city, you can say 'I'm sorry' to someone and never see them again."

Though Canadian publications show more skin than the U.S. media does, Hanmer understood that his cheeky illustration might rattle an old-school paper such as the *Globe & Mail*. Had the paper run it, imagine the mail from Harry in Halifax and Suzy in Saskatoon. There might even have been pressure on the editors to publicly apologize.

When outraged readers grouse about a cartoon and threaten to cancel subscriptions, newspapers often grovel for forgiveness. The *Spectrum*, in Saint George, Utah, did just that in November 2001 after a gaggle of angry readers, some of them aging military veterans, stormed the paper's offices to complain about a cartoon that criticized the war in Afghanistan. The syndicated cartoon by Steve Benson, which ran on Veteran's Day, depicted President Bush as a fighter pilot dropping bombs labeled "killing innocent civilians" and "starving millions of Afghans."

"[The cartoon] should have been printed in Afghanistan, not in America," one *Spectrum* reader griped to the *Salt Lake Tribune*. "They would have appreciated it over there."

The protesters demanded that the *Spectrum* issue a front-page apology. And the paper's editors complied on page one the very next day. Such prominent mea culpas are rare. More commonly, newspapers apologize on the editorial page, as *New York Newsday* did after receiving a slew of letters from readers offended by Doug Marlette's 1994 cartoon mocking the Catholic Church's edict banning women priests.

"While conceived as a critical comment on the recent papal declaration that women can never rise to the priesthood," read the paper's sheepish statement, as quoted in Chris Lamb's book *Drawn to Extremes*, "the cartoon was perceived by many readers to ridicule the pope and the Roman Catholic church. This was not *New York Newsday*'s intention. . . . It is unfortunate, and we regret that many readers were given an unintended message."

In fairness, *New York Newsday* let Marlette write an op-ed defending his cartoon's intended message. He did so eloquently: "It is always bad news when a newspaper apologizes for expressing an opinion—bad news for the First Amendment, bad news for journalism and bad news for readers."

DOUG MARLETTE

Apologized for by *New York Newsday*, 1994

CTON

Killed by the *Globe & Mail*, 2005

2
NOT A PRAYER

IRRELIGIOUS IMAGERY

THE GOSPEL ACCORDING
TO MARLETTE

A wistful Doug Marlette longs for "a different time" when editors who killed cartoons at least agonized over their decision before pulling the trigger. Marlette, who started out at the *Charlotte Observer*, recalls the impassioned newsroom debate surrounding his drawing of Jesus (page 81) schlepping an electric chair on his back as he staggers toward his crucifixion. North Carolina was known as an execution-friendly state, so the cartoon, intended for Good Friday, served as a reminder that Christ too was a prisoner put to death. Marlette's editor spiked the cartoon, but he later wrote about his decision in an editorial that was accompanied, curiously enough, by Marlette's original drawing.

"They were Southerners," says Marlette of his *Observer* editors. "They all came up—'made their bones,' as the Mafia calls it—during the civil rights era. And in the South it mattered what you said. In the Northeast, I found that [free speech] was just an abstraction. It was never tested. In the South it was tested. If you said you didn't believe in lynching, you might get a cross burned on your front lawn. It didn't necessarily mean that these people agreed with a cartoon or that they wanted to run it, but they at least took it seriously."

When Marlette moved up north to work for *New York Newsday* in 1989, he says his editors were quicker to condemn cartoons with religious themes. "*Newsday* was in the Northeast, and run by secular Jews, and the editor was a fallen-away Catholic," says Marlette. "They weren't used to the fluency I had with religious symbols." For instance, *Newsday* turned down a cartoon (page 82) lampooning the decision by the archdiocese of New York to retain a public relations firm. "The idea is so secular and counter to the truths of any religion," says Marlette, who depicted a cardinal in his finery witnessing the crucifixion and musing to a Roman soldier that Christ "should've hired a good P.R. firm." *Newsday* accepted Marlette's second cartoon on the topic, which omitted the crucifixion scene. "I had two guys who looked like cardinals standing in a hallway, and there's a door that says 'Matthew, Mark, Luke and John Public Relations.' And one [cardinal] says, 'No, you tell them we hired another firm.'"

The Pulitzer Prize-winning cartoonist sharpened his knowledge of the Gospels during "sword drills" in Sunday school. "You stand in line and they call out scripture and you look it up," reminisces Marlette. That childhood training has proved indispensable when he tangles with right-wing evangelists such as Jerry Falwell. "When the Jerry Falwells would complain about a cartoon, my secular-humanist, fallen-away [editors] . . . would be bullied, because they kind of didn't believe much and Falwell did. But because of my background, I wasn't intimidated."

DOUG MARLETTE

Killed by the *Charlotte Observer*, undated

DOUG MARLETTE

Killed by *Newsday*, undated

"HE SHOULD'VE HIRED A GOOD *P.R. FIRM!*"

FEAR OF FATWA

Verily the most beloved of you by me, and nearest to me in the next world, are those of good dispositions; and verily the greatest enemies to me and farthest from me, are the ill-tempered.
—Mohammed

I t's safe to say that the sword is mightier than the pen.

On September 30, 2005, Flemming Rose, culture editor of the Danish newspaper *Jyllands-Posten*, ran twelve commissioned cartoons featuring the likeness of Mohammed. His purpose, he later wrote in the *Washington Post*, was to highlight the "widening fears and feelings of intimidation in dealing with issues related to Islam." Rose, now on "permanent vacation" from his paper, went on: "Our goal was simply to push back self-imposed limits on expression that seemed to be closing in tighter."

That experiment has had disastrous results. Frenzied protests filled the streets of many Arab countries, leading to the death of more than 139 people, according to www.cartoonbodycount.com. Mobs torched the Danish embassies in Lebanon and Syria. Palestinian gunmen chased Danish aid workers out of Gaza. Imams in Pakistan placed Salman-Rushdie–style bounties on the heads of the Danish cartoonists, who went into hiding. So great was the fury that outraged Iranian bakers renamed the Danish pastry the "Rose of the Prophet Mohammed."

Thankfully, the tsunami of violence has yet to strike North America. But publishers in the United States and Canada are taking no chances. Whether worrying about upsetting Muslim readers or panicking over the prospect of violent demonstrations outside their offices and the potential costs of increased security, many newspapers and magazines have practically adopted sharia standards in the newsroom. Not only did most major publishers fail to reprint any of the twelve Mohammed drawings, they often belittled them as "juvenile" in editorials and, in some cases, suppressed cartoons criticizing Muslim extremists.

Some cartoonists admit that they, along with their editors, now fear for their safety. "I don't mind admitting that I don't particularly want to look over my shoulder for the rest of my life, or even a week or a month, or have my wife worried about it," says Pulitzer Prize–winning cartoonist Joel Pett.

Randy Bish, of the *Pittsburgh Tribune-Review*, understands that sentiment. "The events of 9/11 have made a lot of editors want to hug their families a little tighter every night as they live in constant fear of reprisal from terrorists," laments Bish, who says his paper viewed his cartoon (page 87) about the wave of violence too incendiary to run in the current environment. "It's a damned-if-you-do, damned-if-you-don't situation," he adds. "Run the cartoons, face protests. Don't run the cartoons, face protests. We must now ask ourselves if risking the possible violence that occasionally accompanies the protests is worth [it]."

"Yes," insists Doug Marlette.

In 2002, Marlette, then with the *Tallahassee Democrat*, posed the question "What Would Mohammed Drive?" beneath a drawing of a man in an Arab headdress at the wheel of a Ryder truck laden with a nuclear bomb. Besides 9/11, the cartoon alluded to Timothy McVeigh's use of a rented Ryder truck in the 1995 bombing of an Oklahoma City federal building, as well as the "What Would Jesus Drive?" campaign by anti-SUV environmentalists. "I didn't think I was drawing Mohammed, but I don't mind if somebody thinks it's Mohammed. When I was drawing it, I was drawing a standard-issue Arab guy," explains Marlette, who says his cartoon decried the distortion of Islam by zealots.

The *Tallahassee Democrat*'s Web site posted the cartoon—but not for long. The Council on American-Islamic Relations (CAIR) orchestrated a protest against the paper. More than 20,000 e-mail complaints flooded the *Democrat*, and Marlette received viruses intended to disable his home computer and vile threats such as, "I will cut your fingers and put them in your mother's ass."

"Those who have attacked my work," Marlette later told *Jyllands-Posten* in an interview, "whether on the Right, the Left, Republican or Democrat, conservative or liberal, Protestant, Catholic, Jewish, or Muslim, all experience comic or satirical irreverence as hostility and hate. When all it is, really, is irreverence. Ink on paper is only a thought, an idea. Such people fear ideas. Those who mistake themselves for the God they claim to worship tend to mistake irreverence for blasphemy."

Marlette's editors were plenty nervous of those who mistake themselves for God; they pulled his cartoon from their Web site and never ran it in the print edition. "We did not publish the cartoon and we won't because I don't think it is particularly funny. And I frankly am uneasy about making fun of religious icons in the *Democrat*," the paper's editor later wrote.

The refusal to publish cartoons confronting the nature of Islamic extremism, argues Marlette, is "one of the low points in the history of

American journalism." Referring to cartoonists as "canaries in the coal mine," he warns that a policy of appeasement will have repercussions. "It's the reason we don't negotiate with terrorists. You encourage the forces of aggression. [Extremists say], 'oh, we want to intimidate newspapers, we just create a big ruckus. We shut down their servers.'"

RANDY BISH

Killed by the *Pittsburgh Tribune-Review*, 2006

MINORITY RETORT

For many years, Khalil Bendib, America's most prominent, if not only, Muslim political cartoonist, veiled his Algerian identity behind the nom de plume Ben Dib. "I was too scared to be Khalil Bendib," admits the Berkeley-based cartoonist and sculptor, who usually uses his full name these days. Revealing his heritage has come at a cost. "I was going to have a show of my ceramics," recounts Bendib. "This local glossy magazine had accepted my work for its cover. The art director, after giving me that false promise, said 'look . . . my publisher feels it's not the right moment with this 9/11 thing.'"

Bendib credits the art director for being candid. Brush-offs can be more ambiguous. He says his normally enthusiastic syndicate, which mainly caters to small town newspapers, found his cartoon Christian Values "too complicated." The editor, ventures Bendib, "probably felt that this might be a little bit provocative to portray any kind of Christians in this light."

The idea for the cartoon bubbled up after Bendib detected a "deafening silence" from the Christian Right following the release of photos of Abu Ghraib prisoners and subsequent shots of a half-naked Saddam Hussein in American captivity. "I never liked Saddam. I'm not sorry for him. I just thought it was in bad taste," says Bendib. "[With] George Bush being ostensibly part of that movement—always asking, 'What would Jesus do?'—I thought this was a good opportunity to point out the hypocrisy of super-Christians doing these super-unchristian things in the name of Jesus Christ."

The photos of naked, blindfolded detainees reminded Bendib of his youth as a refugee from Algeria's war of independence. "I had two uncles who were tortured. One died. . . . We just barely escaped. It was formative. Without that, I would not be political. I'd be doing animation in the Disney studios."

Though Bendib champions free speech, he deplores the controversial Danish cartoons depicting Mohammed—which many Muslims consider sacrilegious. "Every time we pick up a pen, we think of the consequences of what we're doing," says Bendib, who likens the publication of the Mohammed cartoons to yelling fire in a crowded theater. "Freedom is . . . not an absolute. It comes with responsibility."

Although Bendib also denounces protestors who resort to violence, he understands the underlying rage that many Muslims feel. "You are talking about a Third World people who for hundreds of years have been subjected to colonialism. It sounds like not such a big affair, but colonialism is a horror. It dehumanizes you. It humiliates you, day in, day out. Humiliates your values. When you have that as a backdrop, and on top of that comes some nonsensical, stupid cartoon, it's like salt rubbed into a wound."

KHALIL BENDIB

Killed by Minuteman Media, 2005

MAN IN THE MIDDLE

R. J. Matson usually gets hate mail *after* he draws a controversial cartoon, not *before*. That changed when embers from the firestorm sparked by the Danish Mohammed cartoons drifted across the Atlantic and singed some of the readers of the *St. Louis Post-Dispatch*. "I've rarely been in a position as a cartoonist that readers are writing, demanding I say something and calling me a coward," says Matson. Many readers actually challenged the *Post-Dispatch* to reprint the Mohammed cartoons while beseeching Matson "to stick it to Islam."

The issue was not clear-cut to Matson: "The violence is horrible and should be condemned, but it was a stupid provocation to do those images." Cartoonists, he argues, should respect the taboos of different cultures. Matson doesn't hesitate to draw Jesus, because so many churches display his likeness in paintings, whereas, "I can say anything I want about radical Muslim extremists and imams and Middle Eastern politicians and riots without drawing Mohammed."

Anything? In the current atmosphere, many fearful publishers have

91

been interpreting freedom of the press to mean the freedom *not* to publish. Matson, like many of his fellow cartoonists, describes the mood in the newsroom of late as "general skittishness." For instance, his publisher asked to review all cartoons about the cartoon controversy, an unprecedented step. Matson's first stab at a cartoon on the topic (page 94) took aim at both protestors and provocateurs. He created an ad for "Fatwa Art Instruction Schools," the kind of establishment that markets itself on the back of matchbooks ("When I was a kid, I sent in a drawing but I didn't hear back," says Matson with a laugh). Despite its lack of *jihad*-provoking images, the art school cartoon failed to make the grade at his paper, which decided not to reprint the Danish Mohammed cartoons either.

Matson's ambivalence about the conflict deepened. Radical imams seemed to be using the cartoons to incite riots fueled by other long-standing resentments. He heard that, to whip up the crowds, imams were manufacturing and circulating more inflammatory cartoons than the "Danish Dozen" published in *Jyllands-Posten*. Indeed, as Nat Hentoff writes in the *Village Voice*: "The three cartoons that have most enraged Muslims around the world were not among the original 12 in the Danish newspaper. Imams in Denmark toured the Middle East with these additional cartoons—Muhammad as a demonic pedophile; Muhammad with a pig snout; a Muslim at prayer raped by a dog—to show, they said, the degree of hatred in Denmark of Muslims."

But the fury of the protestors nevertheless felt remote to Matson. "[Americans] haven't had filmmakers killed on the street. We haven't had authors go into hiding. It really hasn't happened in this country, and the editors and publishers aren't feeling the same way as they are in Europe. There's not this urgency to take a stand."

Yet "testy" e-mails from readers continued to pour in. To sum up his position on the culture clash, Matson responded with Suicide Cartoonists (page 95). Again, his paper expressed reluctance to print the cartoon, only to relent after Matson made the case that readers expected him to have *some* opinion about a page-one story about cartoons. "The cartoon was my answer to the people asking me to draw a cartoon with Mohammed in it. They are putting me up to fight their battles for them and risk a fatwa . . . Like suicide bombers are pawns in a bigger game. People are asking cartoonists to be a pawn in this game."

R. J. MATSON

Killed by the *St. Louis Post-Dispatch*, 2006

R. J. MATSON

Published by the *St. Louis Post-Dispatch*, 2006

VOYAGE OF THE DAMNED

In his 2003 book *The Courage to Be Catholic*, George Weigel praises the press to high heaven. "Because of the press, some sexual predators have been arrested and jailed. . . . Because of the press, the Catholic Church has been forced to recognize that it is in more trouble than its leaders and lay people might have imagined." Weigel goes further, suggesting that the newspapers that uncovered sexual abuse by priests had help in high places. "If God could work through the Assyrians in the Old Testament, God can certainly work through the *New York Times* and the *Boston Globe* today."

For years, God must have been busy working on other stories. Veteran columnist Jimmy Breslin, author of *The Church That Forgot Christ*, believes that many in the media "genuflected" instead of taking on the church. "For a long, long time, the top five jobs in the [New York] police department had to be cleared through the cardinal," says Breslin, illustrating the church's power. "Supposing you went out and did a billion dollar job investigating [the church], no place in the world would [have] run the fucking thing."

Even after stories about sex crimes by priests have become common-place, publications across the political spectrum continue to treat the church with reverence. The somewhat liberal *Hartford Courant*, for instance, had no passion for Bob Englehart's timely cartoon (page 98) aimed at the post–John Paul II Vatican. "The debate was going on about the Vatican having a black pope. And the debate was going on about having an American pope. I thought, hey, we can have both."

The conservative *Pittsburgh Tribune-Review* scrubbed Randy Bish's 2002 cartoon about Cardinal Bernard Law (page 99) who was accused of covering up for pedophile priests during his many years leading the Boston Archdiocese. "[Editors] were afraid of offending Catholics," admits Bish, who says his devout former boss "had very strong ties" to the church.

Internal politics at the right-of-center *St. Paul Pioneer Press* reportedly sank Kirk Anderson's magnificent cartoon about the Vatican's abandonment of abuse victims (page 100). After a long chill in church-newspaper relations, the *Pioneer Press* had recently reprinted an essay by Archbishop Harry J. Flynn, "which got us in good graces," explains Anderson. "Doing the cartoon would rock that boat." Any cartoon about the church also guarantees a load of angry e-mails. "When I have done cartoons about the Catholic Church, I generally get e-mails like 'You'd never say this [about] Jews.' My response is, 'If Jews were raping small children, I'd still be against that.' "

Anderson gets no glee from pointing out the church's troubles, but he believes that such a big issue demands his attention. Hiding the exploitation of children by priests is "black and white; there's rank hypocrisy, and an abuse of power. A lot of times an issue is complicated, and here it was lacking nuance, which for a cartoonist is a gift."

BOB ENGLEHART

Killed by the *Hartford Courant*, 2005

RANDY BISH

Killed by the *Pittsburgh Tribune-Review*, 2002

KIRK ANDERSON

Killed by the *St. Paul Pioneer Press*, 2002

HEAVEN HELP YOU

You know that Pope John Paul II got a sweet sendoff when the right-wing Media Research Center praised the press for giving the late pontiff a "generous farewell." In press tributes to the pope, most cartoonists portrayed John Paul II as little short of saintly. But even these sympathetic treatments could cause editorial queasiness. Graeme MacKay—who believes that the politically powerful papacy normally warrants satire—seated John Paul II's avatar in a heaven-bound Popemobile (page 103). This innocuous image, says MacKay, struck Ontario's *Hamilton Spectator*, a paper in a heavily Catholic city, as too whimsical. MacKay might have fared better if he, like so many of his colleagues, had sped the pope right to the pearly gates. "At one of our conventions, someone stood up and said a cartoonist should only be allowed to do six pearly gates cartoons in one's lifetime," says MacKay. "I've done about four now. My colleagues joke 'Don Knotts died, I guess you've got to do your pearly gates cartoon.' I'm being careful. . . . I still have two left."

As for John Paul II's successor, cartoonists tended to welcome Benedict XVI, but with some reservations; it was frequently pointed out that John Paul's grim-faced, conservative successor had a tough act to follow. At the same time, few cartoonists, if any, brought up Benedict's past membership in the Hitler Youth. J. D. Crowe, of the *Mobile Register* in Alabama, did his share of drawings honoring John Paul, but by the time of Benedict's election he "was tired of being too reverent. My publisher wasn't quite as ready for the irreverence as I was," says Crowe. His stark caricature of "Old White Guy the Two Hundred Umpteenth" (page 104) spoke to those who had hoped in vain for "an open-minded pope, a little fresh air."

Crowe, who drew a comic strip in college called *Real Papal,* which imagined a John Paul coping with campus life—"He's doing his laundry, and he's got his robes and sheets in his basket"—vows to continue scrutinizing Benedict's reign: "Just because he's the pope, he doesn't get a free ride."

GRAEME MACKAY

Killed by the *Hamilton Spectator*, 2005

POPE JOHN PAUL II

J. D. CROWE

Killed by the *Mobile Register*, 2005

POPE BENEDICT XVI
(a.k.a "Old White Guy the Two Hundred Umpteenth")

THE FIRST
COMMANDMENT
OF CARTOONING

THOU SHALT NOT have fun with the Ten Commandments when illustrating an article for a Jewish newspaper about sexual misconduct by rabbis.

FLASH ROSENBERG

Killed by the *Forward*, 1996

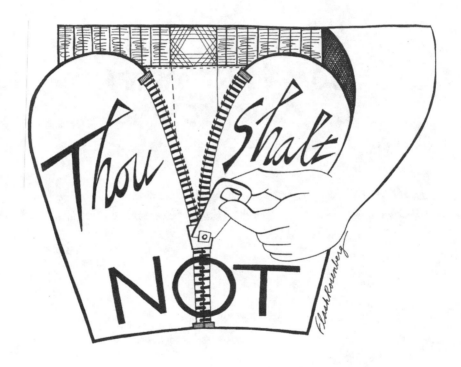

THE FUNNY SOLUTION

How much time does it take to heal a gaping wound like the Holocaust?

Stephen Spielberg's epic movie *Schindler's List* prompted *Hartford Courant* cartoonist Bob Englehart to wonder whether readers might be ready for a dose of Holocaust humor. They weren't, decided his editor.

Sounding very Zen-like, Englehart says he intended "Schindler's *Other* List" to "balance a very serious thing with a very mundane thing." And by doing so, Englehart—who "can't think of anything that should be off-limits for a joke"—tapped into a wider trend. Making the Nazi jokes of *The Producers* seem tame, *Seinfeld* tested the tolerance for Shoah shtick. In one scene that stretched the boundaries of sitcom humor, Jerry and his date were caught canoodling during a screening of *Schindler's List*—a moment that Tom Shales, TV critic of the *Washington Post*, called "one of the most unfortunate 'jokes' in the series."

But essayist Stephen Vider, writing for nextbook.org, felt liberated by the infamous make-out session: "The joke rings true. . . . *Schindler's List* still feels less like a night at the movies than a moral obligation. It's not just mothers like Helen Seinfeld—'You have to see it,' she tells Jerry—who made *Schindler's List* a pseudo-sacred event: Spielberg frames the film in religious ritual, beginning with the lighting of the Sabbath candles and ending with the surviving Schindler Jews placing rocks on Oskar Schindler's headstone."

As Vider points out, Larry David, the cocreator of *Seinfeld*, continued having fun with—or making fun of, depending on one's perspective—Holocaust survivors on his HBO series *Curb Your Enthusiasm*. At a dinner party in one episode, a character who appeared on the reality TV show *Survivor* gets into a deprivation pissing match with Solly, an elderly concentration camp survivor:

> *Survivor* character: "I'm saying we spent forty-two days trying to survive. We had very little rations. No snacks."
> Solly: "Vut you talking snacks? Ve didn't eat sometimes for a week, for a month."
> *Survivor* character: "Did you ever see the show?"
> Solly: "Did you see *our* show? It was called the Holocaust."

Proving that nothing Hollywood can dish up is more shocking than the irreverence of real life, a twenty-nine-year-old Israeli comic book publisher by the name of Amitai Sandy is challenging the whole notion of anti-Semitic humor. Roused by the recent decision of an Iranian newspaper to stage a Holocaust cartoon contest (itself a reaction to the controversial Danish caricatures of Mohammed), Sandy declared his own anti-Semitic drawing contest, open only to Jewish artists. "We'll show the world we can do the best, sharpest, most offensive Jew-hating cartoons ever published!" boasted Sandy on his Web site. "No Iranian will beat us on our home turf!"

Daniel Asa Rose, author of *Hiding Places: A Father and His Sons Trace Their Family's Escape from the Holocaust*, sees a deeper, more paradoxical truth in this issue: he considers concentration camp comedy—whether in cartoons or on TV—as a sign of health. "It's an indicator that the bandage is off," says Rose. "The profound wound that is the Holocaust has finally healed, after half a century, to the point where we can expose it to the sunlight of the real world at last. That sunlight will be harsh sometimes, but ultimately it's going to be salutary."

BOB ENGLEHART

Killed by the *Hartford Courant*, 1993

SCHINDLER'S <u>OTHER</u> LIST

Eggs
milk
Coffee
Bread

SPRINGTIME FOR HITLER ANALOGIES

Martha Stewart as Adolf Hitler? Is that a good thing?

The manners maven and petty perjurer recently received the Hitler treatment: "Martha Stewart and Adolf Hitler have surface similarities: perfectionists with an eye for detail, driven by ambition and notoriously heartless. Martha's ruthlessness has been limited to her staff, relatives, and business associates, whereas Hitler—well, you know," ventured writer Joy Press in the *Village Voice*.

As the number of Holocaust survivors decreases, the number of Nazi analogies seems to rise. Donald Rumsfeld likened blustery Venezuelan president Hugo Chavez to Hitler in February 2006. Meanwhile, several commentators on the Left, including cartoonists Ted Rall and Aaron McGruder, have equated Rumsfeld's boss to the Nazi tyrant. In a 2002 *Boondocks* strip by McGruder, young Michael Caesar ruminates, "Some people in other countries are comparing Bush to Adolf Hitler because of his warmongering."

"That's preposterous," shoots back Huey Freeman. "Even I wouldn't compare him to Hitler. I mean, Hitler was democratically elected. Wasn't he?"

There are those who claim that Hitler analogies almost always trivialize his crimes against humanity. But even Abraham Foxman, national director of the Anti-Defamation League and a Holocaust survivor, ranks some mass murderers such as Saddam Hussein in Hitler's league. "It doesn't have to be taboo in all cases," Foxman told the *Washington Post*.

Paul Szep, formerly of the *Boston Globe*, uses Hitler caricatures sparingly, like cartoon chili powder that easily can overpower subtler flavors. In December 1972, when the United States launched the "Christmas Bombing" of North Vietnam, Szep portrayed Hitler as Nixon's wartime consigliere taking a walk-and-talk with two generals. More than thirty years later, Szep's voice sounds raw at the mere mention of Nixon and his cronies. "They destroyed a country, a country that still today is feeling the effects. I felt so strong about it," he seethes, referring to the opposition of the secret bombing of Cambodia that enabled the totalitarian Khmer Rouge to seize the country. Szep recalls that his editor, who usually gave him "a long leash," judged the Nixon-Hitler comparison out of bounds. "It was no-go territory, because the *Globe* had not seen that kind of imagery before," says Szep, who notes that he was the first staff cartoonist in the paper's history. "Hitler was the most vile image I could think of. That's my best rationale for it. What image has no regard for human life?"

PAUL SZEP

Killed by the *Boston Globe*, 1972

"Hell, you're always going to have bleeding hearts who oppose massive bombing"

3

PROFILES IN NO COURAGE

EDITORS PLAYING POLITICS

THE FUHRER'S FUROR

Like a groom reciting wedding vows, the British press baron Lord Beaverbrook promised "complete freedom" to his newly hired star cartoonist David Low.

But as many a bride has discovered, a suitor's vows do not always match a husband's deeds.

When Low agreed to join the *Evening Standard* in 1927, he made his new publisher sign an unprecedented contract that promised total editorial independence. "No one took seriously the announcements that I was to express independent views. . . . Free and regular expression by the staff cartoonist was unheard of and incredible," wrote Low in his autobiography.

During Low's twenty-three-year tenure at Beaverbrook's *Evening Standard*, Low did enjoy far more latitude to upset the establishment than did many of his colleagues. Beaverbrook, a Tory, let his liberal cartoonist ridicule conservatives. On the other hand, Beaverbrook believed in appeasing the Nazis. Low, an ardent anti-Fascist, made the Gestapo hit list because of his relentless mocking of Hitler as a dolt. Beaverbrook delighted in having his journalists, including Low, take shots at leaders across the political spectrum.

But there were limits to the publisher's leniency.

In late 1937, as the Nazis threatened to invade Austria, the *Evening Standard*'s editor warned Low not to "inflame tempers any more than they are already inflamed." Hitler's propaganda chief, Joseph Goebbels, invited British foreign secretary Lord Halifax to meet with him in Berlin. There, Goebbels complained to Halifax that criticism from British columnists and cartoonists, particularly Low, infuriated his thin-skinned boss.

Practically taking marching orders from Berlin, Halifax tried to shut Low up. Halifax appealed to Michael Wardell, an executive at the *Evening Standard*, telling him, according to Low biographer Dr. Tim Benson, "You cannot imagine the frenzy that these cartoons cause. As soon as a copy of the *Evening Standard* arrives, it is pounced on for Low's cartoon, and if it is of Hitler, as it generally is, telephones buzz, tempers rise, fevers mount, and the whole governmental system of Germany is in uproar."

Wardell arranged lunch between the cartoonist and the foreign secretary, and Halifax lobbied Low to lighten up on Hitler. "I don't want to be responsible for a world war," Low replied, according to his account of the meeting. "But, I said, 'It's my duty as a journalist to report matters faithfully, and in my own medium I have to speak the truth. And I think [Hitler] is awful. But I'll slow down a bit.' So I did."

Following his summit with Lord Halifax, Low seems to have tested the *Evening Standard*'s tolerance; he drew "Celebration Dinner" on December 23, 1937, skewering the imperialist ambitions of Fascist leaders in Spain, Japan, Germany, and Italy. The cartoon was spiked, and Low—who publicly denied interference from his patrons—ceased direct attacks on Hitler and Mussolini. He soon introduced readers to a new character, "The Muzzler," an amalgam of both dictators.

Until war broke out between Britain and Germany, Beaverbrook kept his prophetic cartoonist on a leash—one that Low apparently wore without too much fuss. "Low enjoyed beating a drum about his independence," notes Colin Seymour-Ure, coauthor of a biography on the cartoonist. "It increased Low's authority, in an age of autocratic and mercurial British press barons, if he was able to present himself as a cartoonist whose integrity was unimpeachable and who was answerable solely to his own conscience. Also, Low was a considerable showman and a shrewd self-publicist—regarded by some of his former [colleagues] as somewhat on the make."

DAVID LOW
Killed by the *Evening Standard,* 1937

CELEBRATION DINNER.

BUILDING BLOCK

Ⓘn 1996, on the fiftieth anniversary of the hiring by the *Washington Post* of legendary editorial cartoonist Herbert Block, publisher Katharine Graham said, "Herb fought for and earned a unique position at the paper: one of complete independence of anybody and anything."

By that time, Block—who signed his work "Herblock"—had been accorded honors far beyond the wildest dreams of any American political commentator or cartoonist: four Pulitzer Prizes and the Presidential Medal of Freedom, to name only some of the most prestigious.

As Graham noted, however, the cartoonist's independent status at the *Post* was hard-won. A critical early victory came during the 1952 presidential election campaign, which pitted Democratic candidate Adlai Stevenson against Republican hopeful General Dwight Eisenhower. Herblock's cartoons vigorously supported Stevenson, a stance that angered then–*Post* publisher Phil Graham, whose editorial page had endorsed Eisenhower.

Graham ordered the offending cartoons dropped. "Naughty Naughty," drawn for publication on October 29, 1952, about a week before Election Day, is typical of Herblock's efforts during the campaign. He considered Eisenhower too tolerant of the hardball political tactics of his running mate, Richard Nixon, and Republican hatchet man Senator Joseph McCarthy. This cartoon, with three others, was dropped by the *Post*, but it was sent out as usual for syndication, per an informal agreement between Block and Graham.

Deprived of their daily dose of Herblockian wit and wisdom, enraged *Post* readers accused the newspaper of censorship and demanded the cartoonist's reinstatement. The rival *Washington Daily News* gleefully ran an editorial about the incident. Phil Graham soon relented, and Herblock returned to the pages of the *Post*. As Kay Graham later recalled, "Since the cartoons ran elsewhere in syndication, this ploy was not only ineffective but embarrassing."

In his autobiography, Block recalled the denouement in typically understated fashion: "Phil decided that since everyone knew about our divergent views, and since differing views were, in fact, what distinguished the *Post* from papers where staffers took orders from the chief, it was silly to leave out the cartoons. A few days later they reappeared. After the inauguration, the cartoons still did not give President Eisenhower the support he generally received from the *Post*."

Phil Graham had unwittingly set Herblock free, making him arguably the most independent cartoonist working for a major newspaper that America has ever known. Herblock went on to challenge Joe McCarthy, bedevil Richard Nixon as vice president and later as president, help uncover Watergate, and inspire legions of American editorial cartoonists. He proved the power of one man to make a difference through a lifetime dedicated to journalistic integrity and independence.

Text about Herbert Block written by Harry Katz, curator of the Herb Block Foundation Collection.

HERBLOCK

Killed by the *Washington Post*, 1952

"NAUGHTY NAUGHTY"
October 29, 1952

LOCAL HERO

George Fisher was middle-aged when he started cartooning professionally for a small weekly newspaper in Little Rock, Arkansas, in the 1960s. The cartoons provided an outlet for his rage over the effort of the state's governor, Orval E. Faubus, to thwart the integration of Little Rock schools in defiance of federal court orders. Fisher, who had drawn cartoons for his regimental newspaper during World War II, and Faubus were among a band of veterans who had returned stateside dedicated to throwing out the old political machines and installing a liberal democracy in one of the most reluctant states of the old Confederacy. Fisher contributed cartoons to Faubus's first race for governor in 1954, when that son of a socialist hill farmer upset the conservative incumbent, Francis Cherry. The election turned upon Governor Cherry's attempt to capitalize on the revelation that Faubus had attended a tiny Marxist self-help school in 1935. Fisher's cartoons, published in political ads, skewered Cherry and helped elect Faubus. Three years later, Faubus's deployment of National Guard troops to prevent nine black children from attending Little Rock Central High School made him the most popular politician of his time but alienated reformist supporters such as Fisher.

Faubus's opportunism provoked Fisher to return to political cartooning. His cartoons ultimately found their way into the liberal *Arkansas Gazette*. (The statewide paper later hired him as its full-time editorial cartoonist.) Faubus, who would serve six terms, was Fisher's most familiar subject.

Though Fisher became one of the state's best-known commentators, he resisted syndication, which would have brought him more fame but likely diluted his ability to influence local issues. He didn't believe that his reliance on bucolic metaphors from his rural rearing, which created a strong bond with Arkansas people, would resonate with urban readers.

The accompanying cartoon, which shows Faubus as a monkey, is something of an aberration. Though the *Arkansas Gazette* was a fierce editorial critic of politicians such as Faubus, who tried over the decades to keep evolution from being taught in public school classrooms, the paper did not publish the monkey cartoon. The *Gazette* had never published a caricature of a politician as an animal, and the editor thought it would seem disrespectful to characterize the paper's number-one enemy that way. The editor would regret that decision upon reflection, and many subsequent Fisher cartoons disgraced the animal kingdom with the facial characteristics of machinating politicians.

Text about George Fisher written by Ernest Dumas, a reporter at the Arkansas Gazette *for thirty-one years.*

GEORGE FISHER

Killed by the *Arkansas Gazette*, undated

I'm Not Yet Ready To Accept Evolution

EXPLOSIVE CARTOON

On Pearl Harbor Day 1993, Secretary of Energy Hazel O'Leary dropped a bomb on America. She confirmed that during the Cold War the U.S. government conducted horrific radiation experiments on human guinea pigs.

O'Leary went public only after an exposé in the *Albuquerque Tribune* identified unsuspecting hospital patients who had been injected with plutonium by government scientists. Once only numbers, the victims now had names and faces. More revelations of nuclear depravity soon surfaced, outraging cartoonist Dennis Renault of the *Sacramento Bee*.

A veteran of the army as well as the antinuclear movement, Renault used the revelation of the secret radiation experiments to explore the morality of the atomic bombs dropped on Hiroshima and Nagasaki. He considers the blasts "a form of terrorism because . . . it was an attempt to bring a government to its knees based upon the devastation of civilian populations."

Renault—who says his normally supportive editor worried that his sketch would infuriate veterans—believes that his paper had no stomach for challenging "the conventional thinking" that dropping nuclear bombs was a moral act because it forestalled an invasion of Japan and saved the lives of American soldiers. "That would have been plowing new ground to go back and look at the atomic bomb and think 'God, maybe we were experimenting on these people,' " says Renault.

Had his cartoon been published, Renault doubts that many readers would have reassessed America's decision to drop the bomb, but winning converts, surprisingly, was never Renault's primary objective as a cartoonist. "You are generally preaching to the choir. I don't find that disconcerting or onerous at all. I don't think anybody picks up an editorial cartoon and thinks 'Yeah, I'm going to vote this way.' What I think happens is the troops hear that mortar shell . . . landing on the enemy. It bucks up the troops more than anything else."

DENNIS RENAULT

Killed by the *Sacramento Bee*, 1993

DEATH SENTENCE

"**I** see a lot of violence," says Marshall Arisman between long drags of a cigarette in his Chelsea studio. "Bump somebody on the subway. People are going *off.*"

Arisman, a slim man with white hair, channeled this smoldering rage when he painted a man morphing into a skull (page 132) for *Time* magazine. "The skull has been overused in art, but I thought if I could blend it with a living face that maybe I could get a human emotion out of it." His editors, remembers Arisman with a resigned chuckle, pulled the plug on the image, judging it "too violent" for a cover on the death penalty.

Support for the death penalty was reported by the Gallup Organization in October 2005 at 64 percent, its lowest level since the U.S. Supreme Court reinstated capital punishment in 1976. "Whoever they are polling are not telling the truth," scoffs Arisman, who argues that most Americans cheer executions as an attempt to "remind you that you have power."

Arisman, an opponent of the death penalty who nevertheless understands the appeal of retribution, remembers when his own life was out of control. Long ago, he found himself consumed by road rage, an experience that influenced his painting for *Time*.

"I once almost killed somebody," Arisman confesses. "I was on a road, a country road. The guy [ahead] of me was a hot dog. It was a two-lane highway and he would slow down and I would pull out to pass him in the other lane and he would speed up and my car was not fast enough to get in front of him. I'd slow down and he'd slow down. And he kept me in that second lane until a truck was coming in the other direction. . . . I went off the side of the road in a ditch and I went absolutely nuts. I drove over lawns. I drove through an amusement park. I could see his car. He pulled into a little restaurant. . . . He parked in the parking lot and so I pulled my car behind him and blocked him. And then I got a wrench out of my car. If I had gotten my hands on that guy in that moment I would have killed him. He locked both doors and I smashed both windows and smashed his headlights, and I pulled him out of the car but I had gotten a little sanity back. Had I gotten him two minutes before I would have killed him. It is within my capacity to do this.

"Actually, I believe it is within everybody's capacity."

MARSHALL ARISMAN

Killed by *Time* magazine, 1984

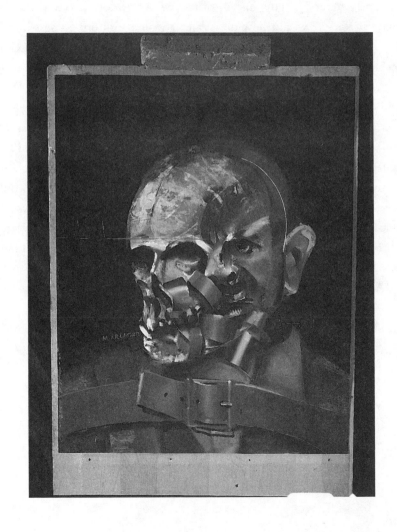

ABORTION SMITES

In *Doonesbury*'s infancy, Garry Trudeau conducted marketing research to map the range of issues that he could and could not get away with. According to *Newsweek*, one of the newspaper editors who replied to a questionnaire designed by Trudeau gave the fledgling cartoonist some guidance: "It has nothing to do with subjects, it's how you execute it." That advice, Trudeau later told *Newsweek*, "opened up a world to me, and I felt if you bring a certain amount of taste and judgment, there's *nothing* that can't be addressed in comic strips."

Well, there is *something*: abortion. Since the debut of *Doonesbury* in 1970, the only strips that United Press Syndicate has refused to distribute parodied the 1985 antiabortion film *The Silent Scream*, which purports to document the pain suffered by an aborted fetus. The six strips (two of which follow) show scenes from *Silent Scream II: The Prequel*, briefly starring Timmy, a twelve-minute-old embryo. "We felt that any number of papers might have a problem with these particular strips on the comics page," Lee Salem, editorial director of Universal Press Syndicate, put it to the *Chicago Tribune*. Trudeau agreed to "withdraw" the Silent Scream send-up, which instead ran in the *New Republic*.

Like Trudeau, M. G. Lord, formerly cartoonist at *New York Newsday*, recalls that editors discouraged her from delving into religious issues, including abortion, which—she admits—is "so complicated that it does not lend itself to simple graphic messages." Yet her simple caricature of the late New York cardinal John O'Connor (page 138)—nixed by *Newsday*—brilliantly captures the antiabortion fervor of a prelate who demonized pro-choice supporters.

In recent years, support for legal abortion has waned, which Lord attributes to the increasing power of Christian fundamentalists. "We, like the good citizens of Iran, live in what is amounting to a theocracy," she says. According to a 2006 Zogby poll, just 52 percent of Americans favor abortion rights.

The antiabortion forces—rebranded as the sunnier sounding "pro-life" movement—deserve their due for relentless and effective proselytizing. But they have had help spreading the message. An analysis by the *American Prospect* found that from March 2004 to March 2006, the *New York Times* op-ed page went out of its way to give a platform to foes of legal abortion. "Not one op-ed discussing abortion on the op-ed page of the most powerful liberal paper in the nation was written by a reproductive-rights advocate, a pro-choice service-provider, or a representative of a women's group," reported the *Prospect*. "Instead, the officially pro-choice *New York Times* has hosted a conversation about abortion on its op-ed page that consisted almost entirely of the views of pro-life or abortion-ambivalent men, male scholars of the right, and men with strong, usually Catholic, religious affiliations. In fact, a stunning 83 percent of the pieces appearing on the page that discussed abortion were written by men."

The fawning coverage received by Supreme Court justice Samuel Alito—who hatched a detailed plan to gut *Roe v. Wade* while working in the Reagan administration—offers another example of the media's flagging support for reproductive rights. The Center for Media and Public Affairs found that 56 percent of the press coverage about Alito's nomination was positive.

"The media falls all over themselves to appear balanced," says Mikhaela Reid, a member of a small sorority of successful women cartoonists. (Only three women—Signe Wilkinson, Ann Telnaes, and Etta Hulme—are nationally syndicated. M. G. Lord left the industry.) Even one of Reid's clients, an alternative weekly in Rochester, New York, rejected a strip about the morning-after pill. The idea for Every Sperm Is Sacred (page 139) was formed in Reid's pro-choice knitting group—"which sounds hippie and granola but it's not. It's a mini–women's think tank."

The strip reflects Reid's anxiety about the crusade to not only overturn *Roe v. Wade* but to limit the availability of contraception. "They are saying that the morning-after pill is abortion, which it is not. RU-486 is the abortion pill; the morning-after pill is a contraceptive. . . . They are saying that the rights of the sperm and the egg override the rights of the woman."

Reid says that the final panel of her strip, which envisions the forcible impregnation of women strapped to an assembly line, concerned her editors. "[They] told me later they felt the image of women basically being tied up and raped by the Sperminator machine was too reminiscent of a recent murder of a young woman in New York City who went to a bar and was found later tied up and murdered."

Though Reid applauds some "white guy" cartoonists who raise the alarm about the threat to legal abortion in America, she believes that issues such as abortion usually get short shrift from male colleagues. "It is dismissed as a soft issue or a woman's issue. 'Oh you women, drawing your cartoons about abortion.' . . . Often there is this perception that we've come so far [that] women's issues aren't issues anymore."

GARRY TRUDEAU

Killed by United Press Syndicate, 1985

GARRY TRUDEAU

Killed by United Press Syndicate, 1985

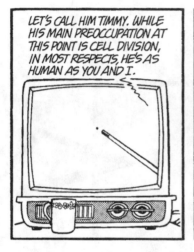

M. G. LORD

Killed by *New York Newsday*, undated

MIKHAELA REID

Killed by the *Rochester Insider*, 2006

MINIMUM RAGE

Covering hard times—as now practiced by the mainstream media—typically means running stories about the legal woes of rappers or the battles that bankers face getting their toddlers into a gold-plated preschool. Dwindling pages are devoted to the plight of actual poor people.

"There is no more telling indictment of reporters and editors than the surprise felt by most Americans in seeing the raw poverty among New Orleans residents after Hurricane Katrina," writes David K. Shipler, author of *The Working Poor: Invisible in America*, in the *Columbia Journalism Review*. "In an open society, nobody who had been watching television or reading newspapers should have been surprised by what Katrina 'revealed,' to use the word so widely uttered in the aftermath."

Editorial art about poverty is also tough to sell to editors, as illustrator Stephen Kroninger found out when the *New York Daily News* spiked his photocollage (page 142). "It's a blue collar paper," says Kroninger, still sounding surprised at the rejection. "You figured it would [resonate] with their audience."

140

It might have. But it didn't resonate with the newspaper's decision-makers, who likely have less in common with the working poor than they used to. A 2002 study by Indiana University-Bloomington found that better educated, more affluent staffers report and edit the news today than in 1971. Perhaps this has had the unintended consequence of creating an empathy gap. If so, we are all the poorer for it.

STEPHEN KRONINGER

Killed by the *New York Daily News*, 2001

LISTENING TO THE AMERICAN PEOPLE

ear for the
working people.

EAR FOR
THE RICH.

PRESIDENTIAL PARDON

Ronald Reagan succumbed to Alzheimer's disease, but after he died in 2004 it was America's cartoonists who suffered from memory loss.

Many cartoonists placed Reagan in heaven or on horseback riding off into the sunset. Forgotten was his dark legacy, including but not limited to: "voodoo economics," the Iran-Contra scandal, ketchup as a vegetable, the invention of "welfare queens," and a deadly indifference to the AIDS epidemic.

Ted Rall, who received more death threats than usual for daring to blog that the just departed president was "turning crispy brown" in hell, believes that the press often treated Reagan with undeserved deference. In 1998, *Time* magazine killed Rall's strip (page 145) that questioned the decision to rename Washington National Airport for Reagan—the man responsible for busting the union representing air traffic controllers. "He already had a free trade building named after him, and I thought that made sense," notes Rall. "But an airport?"

Rall says he had been given the green light to complete the cartoon, but the then top editor of *Time* shot it down at the last moment.

Time also killed Mel Odom's 1980 portrait of Reagan on page 146, which he says editors considered "not paternal enough."

Even during the height of the Iran-Contra scandal, when Reagan's poll ratings ebbed, many in the media polished his Teflon armor, charged Milt Priggee, formerly editorial cartoonist at the *Spokesman-Review* in Spokane, Washington. His editor, for instance, nixed a Reagan-as-Nixon cartoon (page 147). "I thought that cartoon was going to be safe," says Priggee. "There was a public debate going on comparing Iran-Contra with Watergate. Republicans were pooh-poohing it. Liberals were saying 'Here we go again.' "

Despite Priggee's distaste for Reagan—"who made denying empathy respectable"—he argues that the Gipper remains one of the cartoonist's favorite figures to caricature. "Put that hairdo on a traffic light," says Priggee, "and that traffic light was Ronald Reagan."

TED RALL

Killed by *Time* magazine, 1998

MEL ODOM

Killed by *Time* magazine, 1980

MILT PRIGGEE

Killed by the *Spokesman-Review,* 1987

DON'T MESS WITH TEXAS

Put to a vote, many cartoonists and illustrators would elect George Herbert Walker Bush as the most daunting president to draw. Unlike his son, with that trademark smirk, peacock strut, and fondness for cowboy hats, Bush 41 lacked memorable features, walked normally, and wore unremarkable clothes. He could snack on beef jerky, throw horseshoes, and *yeehaw* for the Oak Ridge Boys all day long but never manage to obscure his patrician roots. Garry Trudeau drew Bush 41 as an invisible man, a comment on his understated personality and his role, or lack thereof, in the Iran-Contra scandal during his days as Ronald Reagan's "out-of-the-loop" vice president.

Like Gerald Ford, who suffered for the sins of Richard Nixon, Bush struggled to live down the legacy of the president he succeeded. Steve Brodner's portrait distills Bush's Reagan problem. He poses the ultra-elongated Bush, lips pursed and eyes sunken, front and center before a massive backdrop of a beaming Reagan. "You can hardly see [Bush]," remarks Brodner. "And that to me is the point of the piece. He's hardly there—he's too thin. . . . You notice a thinness that you can exaggerate for the purposes of saying that this man is kind of weak. Weak soup."

Texas Monthly, however, sent back the soup.

The magazine apparently thought better of taking on a newly elected favorite son, even if Bush was born in Connecticut and spent more time in Washington, D.C., than "hometown" Houston. "They had one of their own emerging into the White House, and it was just too much for them," says Brodner. "It was over the line."

STEVE BRODNER

Killed by the *Texas Monthly*, 1988

NO SWEAT

The 2000 Election marked a mid-career crisis for Ward Sutton. "I was outraged. . . . I couldn't believe the way Democrats and liberals seemed to roll over; and the Republicans, by talking louder and bullying, were making [the presidency] happen for Bush. That kind of turned me," says the self-described "recount junkie."

Sutton began his career as an illustrator, striving to get his work published in as many publications as possible. In 1999, he switched to cartooning. "Initially, I had the same modus operandi I had as an illustrator. I would approach magazines and pitch them cartoons that would fit in their niche."

The *New York Times* op-ed page gave Sutton several assignments, and he accepted the paper's unspoken policy to draw presidential candidates even-handedly. "I could not do an anti-Bush or an anti-Gore cartoon. I had to speak to a phenomenon in politics and criticize equally." For example, one Sutton cartoon lampooned how Bush and Gore wooed female voters by appearing on *Oprah*.

As the Florida recount battle intensified, Sutton proposed an "op-art" to the *Times*, a double portrait of the eventual winner, one side gleeful at capturing the White House and the other side asking the question, "At what cost, victory?"

"By definition [op-art] should mean art and opinion combined," points out Sutton. "In reality it doesn't have that much opinion—especially since 2000." The day the Supreme Court declared a winner of the election, Sutton drew an elated Bush mirrored by an anxious Bush with beads of sweat on his forehead (page 154). "The *New York Times* removed the sweat beads from his head, feeling that was too much editorializing," says Sutton. "Everything is so micro-managed. Two little beads on his forehead was saying too much for the paper?"

The sweat-free portrait was not Sutton's only frustration that electoral season. Nine out of ten papers that subscribe to his self-syndicated weekly comic strip refused to publish An Affair to Remember But Not to Recount (page 155).

"Papers e-mailed me saying, 'We can't run this. We'd love to. It's funny, but we're afraid Katherine Harris's lawyers would come after us.' " That was unlikely, Sutton maintains. In satirizing collusion between Harris and Bush, he asks, wouldn't the cartoon represent speech likely to be protected by the First Amendment? Yes, suggests Thomas R. Burke, a partner at Davis Wright Tremaine in San Francisco and a lecturer at the Graduate School of Journalism, University of California, Berkeley. "It is obviously satire to a reasonable reader, and that would be the test." Burke adds that politicians such as Harris or Bush would be unlikely to subject themselves to extensive discovery required in such suits.

Nonetheless, some publications deploy a prevent-defense rather than risk a legal battle—even one they would ultimately win—with a deep-pocketed plaintiff. "Many papers are indeed increasingly concerned about being subjected to any litigation at all. It's a distressing reality," remarks revered First Amendment attorney Floyd Abrams.

Sutton believes that the back-to-back rejections, though exasperating, radically improved his cartoons. "Instead of watering my cartoons down, I make my cartoons as strong as possible and live with the fact that they only appear in certain places."

His strip now pummels Republicans with abandon. Donald Rumsfeld masturbates to scenes of the bombing of Iraq. Dick Cheney and George W. Bush (who frequently looks monkey-like in Sutton's work) go down on men who represent powerful energy conglomerates. And Laura Bush cradles a baby corpse and begs Americans, "Please read to a dead Iraqi child."

WARD SUTTON

Killed by the *New York Times*, 2000

WARD SUTTON

Killed by nine alternative newspapers, 2000

GIVE ME LIBERTY OR
GIVE ME DEATH

Right after September 11, 2001, many cartoonists commiserated with readers instead of commenting on the chaos. On September 12, roughly half of America's cartoonists settled on the same image, the Statue of Liberty in mourning.

"There's been some chatter in the cartoonist community about drawing the Statue of Liberty and how that's cliché, but on that day that's how I felt," explains Patrick O'Connor, of the *Los Angeles Daily News*. He drew Lady Liberty on bended knee, torch dropped, her right hand reaching toward a burning city.

At a time when black smoke enveloped downtown Manhattan and desperate people walked city streets clutching Xeroxed photos of missing loved ones, cartoonists who deviated from offering empathy had trouble getting work published.

Conservative cartoonist Gordon Campbell's vengeful Uncle Sam (page 159) struck editors at the *Inland Valley Daily Bulletin* in Southern California as too harsh. "I thought that would be the sentiment of most readers at the time," says Campbell. "For the first week, I was desiring action."

Overnight, Steve Brodner's cartoon It's A Dangerous World (page 160)," already accepted by the arts journal the *Ganzfield 2* apparently went—in the opinion of editors—from perfect to inappropriate. "I said, 'I beg your pardon, but it's more relevant than ever,' " recalls Brodner. "It's not hard to make nuclear bombs. You can find out on the Internet how to make nuclear bombs. All you need is thirty-five pounds of enriched uranium and nine pounds of plutonium and you can kiss New York or Washington, D.C., or Los Angeles or anyplace else good-bye. Completely good-bye."

Even after the literal and figurative fires cooled, Steve Greenberg noticed a chill in the newsroom of the *Marin Independent Journal.* About a month following the attacks, his editor rejected locked-up Lady Liberty (page 161), a protest against the government crackdown on civil liberties. "[My editor], like many Americans, apparently felt the country and the news media were somehow obliged to not be negative or divisive in a time of national crisis," says Greenberg.

Patrick O'Connor, one of the cartoonists who went through what has been called "Crying Statue of Liberty Syndrome," also regained his urge to defy taboos. His sketch questioning the government's spending priorities borrowed from a famous photograph by Richard Drew that became known as "the falling man." Drew's jarring photo captured a Twin Towers victim who jumped or fell to his death. "That image of people jumping is so personal," says O'Connor. "When the buildings are on fire, it is just pictures of a building on fire. When you see that plane fly in there, it's still just a plane. You know that there are people in it, but you don't actually *see* people."

The mainstream media now shun the Drew photograph, which ran only once in most outlets. O'Connor, whose missile shield cartoon never ran, understands—but disagrees with—that collective decision. Journalists, he argues, sometimes must shock rather than soothe readers, and that's true even during the worst of times. "Everything," he reasons, "should be on the table to look at."

GORDON CAMPBELL

Killed by the *Inland Valley Daily Bulletin*, 2001

STEVE BRODNER

Killed by the *Ganzfield 2*, 2001

STEVE GREENBERG

Killed by the *Marin Independent Journal*, 2001

PATRICK O'CONNOR

Killed by the *Los Angeles Daily News*, September 2001

TAKE-OUT ORDER

Assigned to illustrate an article tentatively entitled "American Excess," Canadian artist Anita Kunz supersized the Statue of Liberty, Uncle Sam, and the American eagle. But the *Los Angeles Times Magazine* had a limited appetite for her treatment of American icons.

Kunz thinks her spiked sketches were insufficiently reverential for the post-9/11 era. "Since September 11th, you have to be a patriot. As President Bush said, 'You are either with us or you are with the terrorists.' That's a hell of a choice, isn't it?" says Kunz.

Magazine editors, suggests Kunz, have been monitoring illustrators more closely in recent years; she misses the days when she had liberty to draw fire from the powers-that-be. Over the years, she's been accused of being anti-woman, anti-Catholic, and anti-Semitic. She has had to fend off a lawsuit, as well as a stalker, because of her provocative paintings. "Twenty-five, thirty years ago it was no problem doing controversial imagery," says Kunz, who admits that she now, on occasion, censors herself. "I could make [George H. W. Bush] really look mean, and I didn't think twice about it. With the son, today, it's really hard to get such things published."

Kunz worries that the next wave of illustrators may not have the freedom, or the inclination, to wield the pen as a weapon. "I teach a lot, and I remember when I was a student we were pissed off and we were interested. Now, you see a lot of looking back, imagery from childhood. It's not about the war. It's not about the administration. I am wondering if students feel a disconnect, no power to change anything."

ANITA KUNZ

Killed by the *Los Angeles Times Magazine*, 2002

ANITA KUNZ

Killed by the *Los Angeles Times Magazine*, 2002

MENACE TO SOCIETY

In rare cases, editorial art has helped shape policy, define a public figure, or spark mass protests. Joe Camel probably tempted more than a few kids to start smoking. That said, editors sometimes overstate the influence of imagery to justify killing a work that makes *them* uncomfortable. An amused Sam Gross recalls that an editor at *Science Digest* worried that the cartoon on page 169 might coax impressionable readers to hack into computer systems.

According to Hal Mayforth, whose sketch (page 170) about the proliferation of spam was deleted by *IEEF Communications Magazine*, editors have become increasingly touchy about publishing symbols of "cartoon violence" such as the round bombs once favored by Boris of *Rocky and Bullwinkle* fame. "You can't get a gun in an illustration unless the story is about a gun," says Mayforth.

The *Sydney Morning Herald* in Australia evidently worried that readers would rush out and join a jihad if exposed to Phil Somerville's cartoon (page 171). A frustrated Somerville sent the rejected photocollage, a visual meditation on " the repetitiousness of human behavior," intended to mark the first anniversary of the World Trade Center attacks, to a TV show called *Media Watch*. The show asked Somerville's editor, Andrew Hornery, to defend his decision to kill the cartoon. "It was inciting hatred against America," Hornery contended.

Media Watch posted Somerville's cartoon as well as his editor's comments on its Web site and invited viewers to weigh in on the controversy. The results hardly vindicated Hornery; the cartoon did incite vitriol— but little of it was directed at America. "One cannot help but wonder why the illustration was censored," wrote one reader. "Does Andrew Hornery fear reprimand from the Ministry of Love? Or perhaps he is also employed at MiniTrue, as an agent of the Thought Police."

SAM GROSS

Killed by *Science Digest*, 1985

HAL MAYFORTH

Killed by *IEEF Communications Magazine*, 2003

PHIL SOMERVILLE

Killed by the Sydney Morning Herald, 2002

The more things change...

THE JOKE'S ON WHO?

Did you hear the one about the 9/11 victims? Probably not. 9/11 inspired few jokes to tell at the watercooler.

Americans were understandably gloomy following the first significant attack on the country since Pearl Harbor. *Vanity Fair* editor Graydon Carter declared "the end of the age of irony," a remark amplified by many in the media.

J. P. Trostle, then cartoonist at the *Chapel Hill Herald*, suggests that the proximity of the attacks to the nation's media capitals heightened the hyperbole. "Humor had been declared dead, and I knew that wasn't true," says Trostle. On the evening of September 11, he stopped at his favorite bar expecting to drink in "stunned silence." But the bar was hopping. "It was trivia night," remembers Trostle. "There was a packed bar of Duke students, and the TV showed the picture of the Towers falling over and over again. I looked around the bar, and it was as if nothing had changed. People were playing trivia. People were getting drunk."

Trostle waited a month after the attacks to test out topical humor, parodying a plan by local officials to tighten security to discourage revelers from attending the city's annual Halloween street party. "People were not allowed to wear their costumes into town. They had to be searched first. . . . It was almost irrational," says Trostle. "*Everything* was a target after 9-11 in America?"

To lobby for his cartoon, Trostle took the "newsroom walk," where he showed sketches to editors and reporters to build support for an edgy idea. "The first thing they did was laugh at it," says Trostle. "The second thing they did was [say], 'We are never going to run this.' "

Trostle laughs off the rejection, but he calls for more—not less—black humor to brighten dark days. "It's part of the survival instinct that humans need to get through tough times."

J. P. TROSTLE

Killed by the *Chapel Hill Herald*, 2001

LIMITED BREATHING SPACE

The death of so many people on September 11, 2001, overshadowed—understandably—the environmental toll of the World Trade Center attacks. According to the Natural Resources Defense Council, the destruction of the Twin Towers released between 300 and 400 tons of asbestos as well as 130,000 gallons of oil contaminated with PCBs. Many first-responders now suffer from respiratory ailments.

The *New York Daily News* aggressively reported on the attack's environmental impact—at first. But the *News*—owned by one of New York's wealthiest real estate developers, Mort Zuckerman—softened coverage of Lower Manhattan's unhealthy air, because, as Cynthia Cotts later reported in the *Village Voice*, editors "buckled under pressure from federal and local authorities." By late September the paper editorialized that environmental reviews—"red tape"—should not slow the rebuilding effort. The paper also killed several columns about the topic by its star reporter, Juan Gonzales, who later told the *American Prospect*: "In twenty-five years as a reporter, I've never faced as much scrutiny or as much difficulty getting stories in the paper as I have had around this issue."

Artist Stephen Kroninger, who had been contracted to create biweekly photocollages for the *News* just before 9/11, had read the paper's environmental reporting right after the attacks. He used a quote from the paper in the caption accompanying the opposite illustration. "They ran a story about Stuyvesant High School, about how bad the air quality was," says Kroninger, whose friend Art Spiegelman had a daughter attending the high school. "Art told me, 'They are putting these kids back in school and they don't know what these kids are breathing.' "

The paper ran Kroninger's illustration but without the caption from its own pages. "Without the caption it was vague, murky. It didn't mean anything," says Kroninger, who stopped contributing to the *News* once he realized that the environment at the paper was hostile to the truth.

STEPHEN KRONINGER

Killed by the *New York Daily News*, 2001

ARIEL ASSAULT

Just before the United States invaded Afghanistan, the Bush administration scrambled to line up Arab support for the war by pushing Israel to play nice with the Palestinians. Israeli prime minister Ariel Sharon shoved back—hard. "Do not appease the Arabs at our expense," barked Sharon in remarks to reporters. "It is unacceptable. Israel will not be another Czechoslovakia. We will defend ourselves."

Comparing British appeasement of the Nazis with the United States bid to win Arab backing for the war in Afghanistan angered the White House, which called Sharon's remarks "unacceptable." The spat between allies spurred many readers to write the letters page of the *Los Angeles Times*, which in turn asked Roman Genn to caricature Sharon.

A proud Zionist and a self-described neocon, Genn depicted the Israeli prime minister as Winston Churchill, replete with V sign, bow tie, and big cigar. "I reduced [Sharon's] weight slightly, because I had sympathy for what he was going through," admits Genn. But the drawing provoked little sympathy from his editor, who—Genn says—told him, "We will not give [Sharon] any favorable light."

Though Genn fervently supports the press's right to mock politicians—you should see his caricatures of the late Yasser Arafat as a frog—he nevertheless complains that cartoonists in the West reflexively drew Sharon as a monster: "He was usually portrayed eating the dove of peace with feathers sticking out of his mouth." Genn was particularly outraged by the British Political Cartoon Society's decision in 2003 to honor the *Independent*'s Dave Brown for his cartoon of a naked Sharon swallowing the head of a Palestinian infant. The caption read: "What's wrong? Have you never seen a politician kissing a baby?"

Genn thinks he understands why cartoonists frequently vilified Sharon. "I don't think people are comfortable with a Jew defending himself. I think Western, non-Jewish cartoonists . . . have a patronizing view and desire to see the Jew as a Holocaust victim.

"British and French cartoonists," Genn continues, "definitely suffer from post-colonial masochism. They failed in occupying and suppressing rebellions; therefore, when they see *effective* resistance to terrorism, they view it as human rights abuse."

Genn predicts that Sharon's reputation will eventually grow, again citing Churchill as an example. "Look at the press Churchill was getting for many years. People called him warmonger. If you listen to the German civilians who got bombed in Dresden, they will definitely tell you he was a war criminal. History edited it a little and showed him in a more favorable light. Churchill was truly a renaissance person. Sharon was more of a farmer. But they were both fighters against aggression."

ROMAN GENN

Killed by the *Los Angeles Times*, 2001

OVER THERE

Foreign news coverage is becoming a lot more foreign to American news consumers.

The print media, with the exceptions of the *Washington Post*, the *New York Times*, and the *Los Angeles Times*, dedicates far fewer pages than they once did to international stories; the ever-shrinking *U.S. News & World Report* might as well be called *U.S. News and No World Report*. *Time* recently fired its bureau chiefs in Beijing, Seoul, Jerusalem, and Moscow. In 2004, *Newsweek* published 50 percent more cover stories on entertainment than international affairs. According to an annual study of newspapers by the Project for Excellence in Journalism, front-page articles on foreign affairs fell by almost 50 percent between 1977 and 2004. When newspapers and magazines do devote space to foreign coverage, stories usually focus on terror attacks, plane crashes, earthquakes, and wars fought by American troops.

Even wars have trouble competing against vacationing white girls who disappear on Caribbean islands. "Is there a war going on?" asks cartoonist Patrick O'Connor of the *Los Angeles Daily News*. "You wouldn't know it by reading my newspaper. It's buried on the back page." Unlike many cartoonists, O'Connor says his editors much prefer cartoons on local issues to commentary on national or international events. O'Connor's editors, for instance, tossed out the welcome mat that he weaved for Pakistan's strongman Pervez Musharraf, who was coming to town to give a speech. "They call Musharraf the president. But he wasn't elected. Well, he was elected in a Saddam Hussein-style election," says O'Connor. "I understand why he is America's ally, but that does not excuse us supporting thugs, as we have over the course of our history." O'Connor concedes he has limited power to stray from the party line: "I work for a conservative paper, and, ultimately, that means supporting our government's foreign policy."

PATRICK O'CONNOR

Killed by the *Los Angeles Daily News*, 2003

BUSHWHACKED

Just as *Mobile Register* cartoonist J. D. Crowe knows not to tarnish the legacy of Alabama coaching legend Paul "Bear" Bryant in a cartoon—"I'd be looking for other work"—he knows he must tread carefully when criticizing the Bush administration. "This is the Bible Belt. This is also the Bush Belt. So anytime I do a cartoon that questions the administration, for the most part it's almost like blasphemy. 'Because you can't question the administration. This is a good, God-fearin' president. . . . He's trying to do the best that he can, and you stay off of him.' "

The *Register*, which Crowe describes as "very, very conservative" on national issues, blunted some of his pointed attacks on the Bush White House and its cronies. In 2003, amid revelations that several baseball stars bulked up with steroids to improve performance, Crowe proposed a cartoon about Halliburton being hooked on no-bid government contracts. "They are getting rich off these contracts, getting fat off of war," alleges Crowe, whose jab at Dick Cheney's former employer was too sharp for management.

The experience of Crowe and other cartoonists (including one who was told, before being fired, that he could dissent from the publisher's conservative policies only on Sundays) debunks the myth of liberal elites as media puppet masters. You hear that claim regularly on top-rated gabfests such as the *O'Reilly Factor* and *The Rush Limbaugh Show*. But if the premise of a leftist-dominated media is correct, would the *O'Reilly Factor* and *The Rush Limbaugh Show* be top rated? And would conservative writers such as Cal Thomas, George Will, and Robert Novak be among the most widely syndicated columnists in America? Would the number of independent-minded editorial cartoonists be dwindling?

To advance their premise that media coverage lurches left, conservative pundits routinely point to surveys showing that a majority of journalists vote for Democratic presidential candidates. But using such polls as evidence of news bias assumes that all Democrats are progressives (rather than fallen Republican moderates) while ignoring the power and politics of the owners of large media corporations—who are hardly the most liberal lot. Media critic Stanley Mieses puts it this way: "Whoever controls distribution controls the business. And so, the fact is the big media conglomerates are AOL, Time Warner, General Electric, AT&T, Disney, Sony, Vivendi Universal, Liberty Media, Bertelsmann, and News Corporation. If there's a hotbed of progressive, liberal thinking in there, I don't see it."

J. D. CROWE

Killed by the *Mobile Register*, 2003

THE L WORD

American reporters sometimes sound like Soviet diplomats when writing about the Bush administration's frequent lies. Euphemisms for the word "lie," notes writer Mike Walsh on the Web site missioncreep.com, include "misstatements," "now-disavowed claims," "falsehoods," "distortions," "faulty" or "dubious" intelligence, "lapses by President Bush," and "the flap over Bush's assertion."

Perhaps the mainstream media takes language lessons from the administration itself. Following Bush's fraudulent claim in his 2003 State of the Union Address that Iraq tried to buy yellow cake uranium from the African nation of Niger, one senior aide remarked that the president "is not a fact-checker."

Mike Luckovich, the Pulitzer Prize–winning cartoonist at the *Atlanta Journal-Constitution*, fears that reporters confuse the public by "fuzzying" up the language they use. "If someone is lying, whether it is a Republican or Democratic politician, say they're lying," pleads Luckovich.

That's easier said than done.

Luckovich's 2003 sketch of military coffins spelling out "W Lied," an expression of his doubts about the official justification(s) for the Iraq War, ended up on his editor's bulletin board. Cynthia Tucker, the *Constitution*'s editorial page editor, told a trade magazine that she thought "it was too early in the war to lay these deaths firmly at the president's feet."

Rick Cole, of the *Trentonian*, suspended suspicions he had about President Bush's honesty after 9/11. "Everybody was behind him. I was behind him," says Cole. Those sentiments changed when, as a pretext to invade Iraq, the Bush administration hyped a link between Saddam Hussein and al Qaeda that did not exist.

In September 2003, after watching the chaos mount in Iraq, Cole submitted a cartoon (page 190) that questioned reports that the administration even had a post-invasion plan. "My editor really liked it, but he said if I wanted to get any national cartoons in [the paper], I might want to stay away from attacking Bush."

Cole marvels at the White House's ability to "spin"—another common surrogate for lying: "They know how to sell their product. . . . They don't come across—to most people—as blatantly corrupt."

During Bush's second term, reporters have become a bit more aggressive in investigating White House whoppers. But a wariness to confront Bush's deceit remains. Consider the Bush administration's no-court-order-required domestic spying program. Here's Bush campaigning in Buffalo, New York, on April 20, 2004: "Any time you hear the United States government talking about wiretap, it requires—a wiretap requires a court order. Nothing has changed, by the way. When we're talking about chasing down terrorists, we're talking about getting a court order before we do so." Rick Cole tried to touch on the subject, sending his readers a wry Christmas card (page 190), which his paper promptly marked "return to sender."

MIKE LUCKOVICH

Killed by the *Atlanta Journal-Constitution*, 2003

RICK COLE

Killed by the *Trentonian*, 2003

RICK COLE

Killed by the *Trentonian*, 2005

SHOOT THE MESSENGER

The "Powell Doctrine"—using overwhelming force to defeat an enemy—was abandoned by the Bush administration in Iraq, but a similar strategy seems to have been deployed in the White House's war on the media.

This war has been waged on several fronts. The president and his surrogates try to undermine the media's credibility with the public by routinely blaming journalists for all the bad news spilling out of Iraq. "There's a constant sort of perception, if you will, that's created because what's newsworthy is the car bomb in Baghdad. It's not all the work that went on that day in fifteen other provinces in terms of making progress towards rebuilding Iraq," complained Dick Cheney in March 2006 on *Face the Nation*.

On the legal front, the Justice Department launched a probe in early 2006 into a *New York Times* exposé of the Bush administration's warrantless domestic surveillance program. A subpoena may be in the offing for *Times* reporters James Risen and Eric Lichtblau, who broke the story.

Such actions undoubtedly skew media coverage of the White House. Lucy Dalglish, executive director of the Reporters Committee for Freedom of the Press, worries that "journalists with smaller news organizations are feeling the chill more than anyone else, because they don't have the big bucks to launch a legal battle if someone tries to either subpoena them or shut them down."

Most disturbingly, Iraq has proved to be the riskiest war in history for journalists. Some reporters have lost their lives to explosive devices and other battlefield weaponry; others were kidnapped by insurgents and later murdered. And some were killed by fire from U.S. troops, inspiring Rainer Hachfeld's cartoon Kill the Press, which he says his editors rejected as "too malicious." Yet malicious might not be too strong a word for the U.S. missile strike on al-Jazeera's Baghdad Bureau that killed correspondent Tareq Ayyoub on April 8, 2003. According to the Committee to Protect Journalists, "Al-Jazeera officials pointed out that the U.S. military had been given the bureau's exact coordinates weeks before the war began." The military claims that American troops were simply returning fire from the building that housed al-Jazeera—a claim that would be more credible had President Bush not discussed attacking al-Jazeera during a White House meeting with British prime minister Tony Blair roughly a year before the war. "He made clear he wanted to bomb al-Jazeera in Qatar and elsewhere," a source told England's *Daily Mirror*. "Blair replied that would cause a big problem."

The big problem, for the media, is an American president who would even *consider* an internationally recognized journalistic enterprise as a target in the "war on terror."

RAINER HACHFELD

Killed by *Neues Deutschland,* 2003

COURAGE UNDER FIRE

Ted Rall's beachscape of death (page 197) was inspired by a report in *Newsday* that U.S. Gulf War veterans might be having some remorse about using tanks outfitted with earthmoving plows to bury Iraqi troops alive. "The image of a Ramones' album cover with a very rollicking Coney Island kind of scene with the Wonder Wheel and the Cyclone popped into my mind," remembers Rall. "I was thinking first about . . . being buried in the sand. I wanted the focus to be on how the vets were dealing with [the atrocities] afterwards. . . . I thought to myself, 'yeah, sure, some of them feel terrible and that's why this is coming out, but most probably don't.'"

Rall and his editor at the now-defunct San Francisco Chronicle Features Syndicate battled over the cartoon. Rall lost. "[The syndicate] said that the cartoon was unfair to the veterans, because they were victims of this policy that had traumatized them. My reaction was that the real victims were the dead Iraqis, and that the people who killed them were in the *volunteer army*. And that still informs my view of the military. These guys are volunteers. And therefore they don't have to be there. They could refuse the order, be court-martialed."

Rall understands the risks of lobbing graphic grenades at the military. His 2004 cartoon (on page 198) that questioned the late Pat Tillman's decision to abandon a lucrative NFL career so he could join the U.S. Army prompted msnbc.com to pull the strip and permanently drop Rall. The *Washington Post*'s Web site also stopped running Rall after the Tillman cartoon.

The Pentagon originally reported that Corporal Tillman, who gave up a $3.6 million contract after 9/11, died heroically in combat during a patrol in Afghanistan in April 2004. In 2005, with reporters debunking the initial account of Tillman's death, the U.S. military changed its story: Tillman was a victim of friendly fire. Then in 2006, the army announced a criminal investigation to determine whether Tillman's death amounted to negligent homicide. Charges persist that military brass knowingly lied about Tillman's death to avert a public relations embarrassment.

Rall, who considers the wars in Iraq and Afghanistan as part of an American plot to control oil, drew a cartoon about Tillman after watching the ultrapatriotic made-for-TV memorial saluting him. He believes that the Bush administration cynically used Tillman as a poster boy for a "death cult."

"As [Tillman's] father said, they tried to turn him into a martyr," says Rall. "There's a bar in San Francisco called Ireland's 32. And you go there and there's all these pictures and posters of IRA martyrs. You walk around the West Bank and you see all these murals of suicide bombers who have gone to meet their virgins in the hereafter. . . . Those are death cults. It's like they're saying death is better than life. . . . Don't try to take care of your family, don't indulge yourself, don't go to the movies. Give up your life for this noble cause.

"[Tillman's] is a cautionary tale. A tragedy," adds Rall. "My best—and, therefore, most controversial—cartoons are always meant to puncture a myth. This was a right-wing myth. Pat Tillman did good. No. Pat Tillman fucked up."

TED RALL

Killed by the San Francisco Chronicle Features Syndicate, 1991

HOW GULF WAR VETERANS LIKE TO SPEND THEIR SUMMERS

TED RALL

Killed by msnbc.com, 2004

RULES OF ENGAGEMENT

Steve Brodner's teenage daughter happened by his drafting table one day while he was illustrating a *New Yorker* article about the Iraq War. The story, entitled "Home Front," chronicled the pain of a father in Iowa who had lost his soldier-son in Iraq.

"What do you think it is?" Brodner asked his daughter.

"Oh, it's real great, Dad," she exclaimed.

"What does it mean?" Brodner persisted.

"Oh yeah," his daughter said. "Lambs to the slaughter."

Brodner knew then that his painting of soldiers arriving in Baghdad, as columns of smoke rise in nearby skies, was in peril. "The consensus was it was way too strong," Brodner remembers his editors telling him. The press pays respect to the troops in peacetime, but when war flares, many in the media cover the military (and the commander in chief) with extreme caution. "And it stays that way for a good long time," says Brodner, "until there's such overwhelming evidence . . . that the war was a mistake and based on lies. Then people can start to really be critical."

The *New York Times* op-ed page, which publishes, arguably, the most potentially influential editorial art in the world, has locked and loaded but held its fire during the Iraq War. When Peter Kuper wired the White House up to the iconic image of a hooded Abu Ghraib prisoner in a crucifixion pose, the *Times* opted for a less striking illustration of an American eagle with a shield like the one on the back of a dollar bill. In one hand, the eagle holds arrows entwined with wires. A bloody handprint soils the shield. "So it didn't end up being a super-light," acknowledges Kuper, "but the direct connection of the wire going to the White House didn't fly. They want to be subtle enough so that they don't get fingers pointed at for, 'Oh, you made that absolute statement,' which is too bad because the op-ed page is made for just that type of thing."

Some editorial cartoonists, too, have had to tiptoe in minefields as more soldiers return home in body bags. According to the *Progressive's* McCarthy Watch column, cartoonist Dennis Draughon of the *Scranton Times-Tribune* was prevented from expressing misgivings about the Bush administration's handling of the Iraq War. During a July 2003 press conference, held as insurgent attacks increased in Iraq, reporters asked Bush if he had any message for America's enemies. "Bring 'em on," the president famously shot back. That belligerent taunt spurred Draughon to depict the president at a podium, declaring "Bring 'em on!!" in front of an "audience" of flag-draped military coffins (page 204). Draughon sent his censored cartoon to an industry Web site, where its appearance prompted several readers to send protest letters to the *Times-Tribune*. The paper, reported the *Progressive*, then issued a strict order to Draughon: no more Bush cartoons.

Draughon later resigned. He prefers not to discuss his paper's actions, but he has plenty to say about the "sanitization" of the Iraq War. He points out that the Bush administration refuses to release photos of military coffins, and the press goes right along with the dictate—a far cry from the Vietnam War. "You couldn't escape it then—body bags and hel-icopters picking up the wounded during firefights. . . . War is a messy business, and I don't think we need to hide that from the folks who are paying the bill for it. We need to know the full cost—and it's not just dol-lars and cents. It's broken lives, broken bodies, and broken spirits."

Draughon wonders if his colleagues have forgotten Vietnam—namely the Gulf of Tonkin incident in which President Lyndon Johnson exagger-ated an attack on a navy ship off the Vietnamese coast to give him the grounds to escalate hostilities. "I'm skeptical anytime our government takes us into war," says Draughon. "I don't think Americans—including cartoonists—question their government enough."

STEVE BRODNER

Killed by *The New Yorker*, 2005

PETER KUPER

Killed by the *New York Times*, 2004

DENNIS DRAUGHON

Killed by the *Scranton Times-Tribune*, 2003

4
FALL FROM RACE

NOTHING IS BLACK AND WHITE

BLOOD AND GUTS

Norman Rockwell's legacy can be measured by one word: *Rockwellian*. Although Orwellian might pop up in conversation more frequently, Rockwellian is commonly understood to refer to the idealized, "aw-shucks" America depicted on many of Rockwell's covers for the *Saturday Evening Post*.

"The nation's favorite father figure," as his biographer Laura Claridge dubbed Rockwell, commanded attention for a good chunk of the twentieth century. His *Four Freedoms* cover paintings demonstrated his influence; a nationwide tour of the patriotic paintings raised $132 million for the war effort. "Norman was a great visual narrator—*Jesus*, could he do story," says art critic Dave Hickey, who credits Rockwell's 1960s paintings on race relations with "mainstreaming the civil rights movement."

But even Rockwell—arguably America's most famous artist—lacked a free hand to confront the civil rights struggle. In an interview with the *International Herald Tribune* in 1968, Rockwell, then seventy-four, admitted that editor Ben Hibbs of the *Saturday Evening Post* limited his choice of subjects. "I remember a time when Ben Hibbs said: 'Anytime you want to, use a Negro. But always put him in the servant's position.'"

Rockwell enjoyed somewhat more artistic freedom when he started working for *Look* magazine. His 1964 painting *The Problem We All Live With*, which shows a young black girl walking past a wall scrawled with racist graffiti as she's escorted to school by four burly federal marshals, achieved iconic status.

Equally emotional, but less known, is *Blood Brothers*. Inspired by *The Dead Matador* by Edouard Manet, Rockwell initially portrayed a black man and his white friend dead in a ghetto. With the war in Indochina raging, *Look* requested that Rockwell substitute a Vietnamese village for the inner city. Rockwell's haunting revision showed two dead marines—one black, one white—in a pool of melding blood. "His idea for the painting," Claridge writes in *Norman Rockwell: A Life*, "was the visual mixing of the blood flowing from both men, reminding the audience that skin color didn't affect the deepest levels of human connection."

Look again passed on the piece, notifying Rockwell that an African American editor at the magazine found the painting "patronizing." The comment wounded Rockwell and led to some self-doubt. But any misgivings about *Blood Brothers* receded in time. According to Claridge, Rockwell ultimately concluded, "*Look* lost its nerve."

NORMAN ROCKWELL

Killed by *Look* magazine, 1968

Photo courtesy of Norman Rockwell Museum, Stockbridge, Massachusetts. Reprinted with permission of the Norman Rockwell Family Agency. Copyright © 1986 the Norman Rockwell Family Entities.

A THIN LINE BETWEEN
LOVE AND HATE

Milt Priggee has had plenty of cartoons killed, but few are spiked twice. When the Washington Redskins reached the Super Bowl in 1988 and again in 1992, Priggee submitted the same cartoon (page 212), knocking the team for its name, which many Native Americans find derogatory. "I had done my own judicious editing, because instead of spades I [originally] had the N-word. And it was unanimous the N-word would overshadow anything I was trying to say," recalls Priggee. "[Even after that change], the editor said, 'We can't run it. This is racist . . . we are going to get mail.' I said, 'Isn't that the reason you hired me?' "

Depicting minorities is like "walking a tightrope," says cartoonist Steve Greenberg. To communicate with readers at a glance, Greenberg, like many cartoonists, uses familiar symbols such as a headdress to identify Arabs. "At the same time, you have to not get into gross stereotypes. If you drew an Asian with Caucasian eyes, it's not going to look like an Asian anymore, but you also need to avoid the World War II imagery [of the Japanese] with buck teeth and extreme slant eyes—the yellow menace."

Greenberg says his editor at the *Marin Independent Journal* booed his balancing act, refusing to publish his "acknowledgment cartoon" about California's booming Hispanic population (page 213). "The circulation of the paper was not growing, and she was very afraid that cartoons might piss off a reader and cause a cancellation," he says.

He defends the choice of *que pasa* as an appropriate replacement for the word *eureka* (Greek for "I have found it") on the state's seal. "It is slang, but I don't think there is anything pejorative about [*que pasa*]. It just means 'What's happening?' I asked Hispanic employees at the paper, 'Does this bother you?' They all said, 'No, it's funny.' "

Asked if he ever regretted a cartoon, Greenberg quickly volunteers a mea culpa: "One in the mid-1980s about Martin Luther King Day, indicating that it was a black holiday and Native Americans were left out. Coworkers of a number of ethnicities approached me after that and said, 'You've missed the point. It's not a black holiday.' I just blew it. . . . My coworkers' comments made me reexamine it. It wasn't a black holiday. It was about acceptance and equality and appreciating the multiethnicity of the country."

MILT PRIGGEE

Killed by the *Spokesman-Review*, 1988, 1992

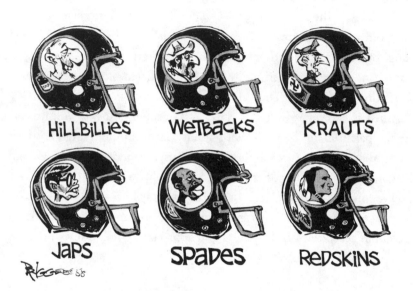

HiLLBiLLies   WeTBacks   KRAUTS

JaPS   SPaDeS   ReDSKiNS

STEVE GREENBERG

Killed by the *Marin Independent Journal*, 2001

THE TIMES THEY ARE
A-CHANGIN'

"**I**t's a thin line between essence-capturing caricature and insulting cartoon, particularly when it comes to race," reads a 2004 *Publishers Weekly* review of *Al Hirschfeld's Harlem*, "so it takes as practiced and bighearted an artist as Hirschfeld (1903–2003) . . . to take on the challenge of depicting historical Harlem."

Hirschfeld's posthumously published book, a mix of lithographs done during Harlem's heyday with subsequent drawings of African American icons, includes a fairly realistic 1996 caricature of Louis Armstrong tooting his trumpet. "If anyone deserved to blow his own horn, it was Louis Armstrong. Pops. Satchmo. Ambassador of Jazz to the World," enthused Hirschfeld in the caption. "What never ceased to amaze you about Armstrong is that he changed not only the way musicians play music (Remember: he all but invented the jazz solo) but the way singers sing (He's the man who invented 'scat singing.')."

Obviously, the great caricaturist revered the great trumpet player. But in 1998, when *Time* magazine commissioned Hirschfeld to draw Arm-

214

strong and several other stars on a cover celebrating "100 Artists and Entertainers of the Century," Hirschfeld sounded an uncharacteristic sour note. Sophisticated Chaplin. Perfect Spielberg. Love the Lucy. Cubist Picasso—*fantastico*. But it's hard to get way away from the fact that Armstrong's face looks somewhat simian, conjuring up verboten racial stereotypes. "There is a long history where blacks are compared to apes, orangutans, or monkeys," explains David Pilgrim, the founder and curator of the Jim Crow Museum of Racist Memorabilia at Ferris State University. "Blacks-as-beasts" caricature, he adds, contributed to an entrenched stereotype of African Americans as subhuman. Pilgrim warns that even well-intentioned artists can create disparaging imagery. "A cartoonist or an artist is not an anthropologist, not a sociologist, but they can do harm inadvertently by tapping into preexisting racial stereotypes."

Hirschfeld rebuffed *Time*'s request for a revision of his Armstrong caricature, but he agreed to draw Bob Dylan as a stand-in for Satchmo on the final cover (Chaplin was also bumped). In his book *Hirschfeld On Line,* he later published the rejected *Time* cover along with remarks brimming with bewilderment: "One of the editors opined that my depiction of the great Louis Armstrong—whom I'd been drawing for decades and unequivocally admired—was less than flattering. You be the judge if the King of Jazz would say I played him false."

Steven Heller, the senior art director of the *New York Times*, who worked closely with Hirschfeld, views the Armstrong flap as an aberration. "Maybe he just stepped over the line by accident, and *Time* knew it," says Heller, who points out that Hirschfeld lived the majority of his life in the pre-*Amos-'n'-Andy* era, a time of different conventions regarding the depiction of African Americans. "There are certain things that an artist does because it's natural to that artist, and not proof that that artist has bias. The bias is in the line. It's not in the head."

AL HIRSCHFELD

Killed by *Time* magazine, 1998

FAIR OR FOUL?

Those offended by John Callahan's cutting cartoons include—but are not limited to—Native Americans, feminists, Asians, Alzheimer's patients, puppy lovers, chiropractors, and that weepy TV pitch-woman for the poor, Sally Struthers. Callahan, who once described himself as "a vulture, feeding off political correctness," relishes criticism; he posts angry letters in a dedicated hate mail section of his Web site. But he faced more scorn than usual when he poked fun at Martin Luther King.

The cartoon made news in 1995 when the *Miami Herald* Sunday magazine, *Tropic*, mistakenly published the King cartoon. An assistant editor had moved the cartoon from the circular file to the publish pile. The *Herald* learned of the flub after the edition featuring the offending cartoon had gone to press but before it had reached newsstands. At a cost of roughly $45,000, the paper destroyed and reprinted more than half a million magazines. Word of the *Herald*'s move leaked out, so to speak. "It was taking the most sacred statement of the aspirations of an oppressed people and tossing it off in a cheap masturbation joke," *Tropic* editor Tom Shroder told the *Washington Post*. The *Herald* then permanently dropped Callahan's syndicated cartoon, punishing him for *its* own error.

Callahan initially battled back in the *Washington Post*: "People are so reactionary and so quick to say you're playing the race card. I'm a big fan of Martin Luther King and very respectful of the black community. The *Miami Herald* hired me to be the politically incorrect cartoonist. I don't understand the inconsistency or the hypocrisy. What in the world is so loaded about this particular cartoon?"

Branded a bigot, Callahan later publicly apologized for hurting people's feelings. Whether an apology was appropriate merits debate. Arthur McCune, writing in the *Ledger* of Lakeland, Florida, defended the cartoon: " . . . Callahan never criticizes King's message or his politics. He simply takes his most eloquent verbal moment . . . and assigns it a more everyday, and slightly salacious, meaning. He reminds us that Dr. King, before he was Dr. King, was a 13-year-old boy named Martin." Michael Eric Dyson, author of *I May Not Get There with You: The True Martin Luther King Jr.*, sees the civil rights leader as a romanticized figure due for demystification. "You don't have to be perfect to be useful," Dyson told the Associated Press. And King himself was not above telling dirty jokes. The FBI taped him laughing with friends about JFK's sex life shortly after the president's assassination.

"I fully expect that King himself would have very much enjoyed [Callahan's cartoon] and found it hilariously ribald," suggests King's Pulitzer Prize–winning biographer David J. Garrow, an opinion seconded by Dr. Ralph Luker, who coedited the first two volumes of King's papers. But Luker cautions that what King might have enjoyed in private could spark his anger in public. "He was fairly protective of any threat to undermine his public status."

Perhaps King would have ultimately taken pride in the cartoon. The fact that humorists try to crack bawdy jokes about African Americans—hazing that Jews and Catholics, Italians, and Polish have endured—might be taken as unorthodox evidence that King's dream is closer to being realized.

JOHN CALLAHAN

Killed by the *Miami Herald*, 1995

KNOCKOUT ARTIST

As an amateur boxer, Tim O'Brien used a crisp jab to outpoint opponents. It's a style he still relies on as an illustrator. But O'Brien tried to land a devastating blow when *Time* magazine asked for his color commentary on the 1997 Tyson-Holyfield rematch—dubbed "the bite of the century."

In the third round, a battered Mike Tyson lost the fight and his composure, biting off part of Evander Holyfield's right ear. "To intentionally foul is cowardly," says O'Brien, a Golden Gloves winner who still sounds palpably disappointed in Tyson, despite the intervening years. "The code is you go down on your shield. . . . That's just how street he is. He'd rather be arrested than be knocked out."

"I did a bunch of sketches—one was [Tyson] as a monster, Frankenstein. Another was him as a cowardly lion," recalls O'Brien, who settled on portraying Tyson as a pit bull. "He's got a great face. The angles of his eyes and the angle of his snarl make a complete X on his face."

Time chose something safer by another artist; O'Brien thinks the magazine balked at depicting a black man as a dog. "There is a pretty poor American history with African Americans, so I understand their hesitancy."

Two years earlier, *Time* had been bloodied for running a controversial cover of O. J. Simpson by photo-illustrator Matt Mahurin, who had altered Simpson's mug shot, darkening his skin to create a moody, menacing portrait. A fury followed. Benjamin Chavis, then head of the NAACP, attacked *Time* for making Simpson look like "some kind of animal."

Time was accused in the press of racism and flouting journalistic ethics, and the genre of photo-illustration went on trial. Many in the media were harsh judges. The words "photo-illustration" were frequently placed in quotation marks normally reserved for hucksterism such as "past life therapy."

O'Brien doubts that his Tyson illustration would have sparked similar protests given the fighter's animalistic behavior in the ring. Yet he recognizes that the legacy of the O. J. cover lingers. "Magazines are much more careful about what they put on the cover than they were ten years ago. Now, maybe every ten weeks is a [cover] illustration, and usually it's for a story about yoga."

TIM O'BRIEN

Killed by *Time* magazine, 1997

MUCH OF A MUCHNESS

In the late 1960s, when Pete Wagner started working in the alternative media, underground papers were "co-ops and collectives," he recalls, "or at worst, very democratically organized corporations that incorporated in name only." The shoestring operations were long on passion and short on profits.

To Wagner, the differences between alternative weeklies and establishment newspapers have been dwindling. The weeklies have become big business. On January 31, 2006, when New Times Media and Village Voice Media merged under the name Village Voice Media, the value of the combined company was estimated at roughly $400 million. The national newspaper chain now owns seventeen publications, including the *Village Voice*, *LA Weekly*, *Seattle Weekly*, *Nashville Scene*, and Minneapolis' *City Pages*, where Wagner worked for ten years.

Like his brethren at daily papers, Wagner sometimes clashed with micromanaging editors at *City Pages*. "Weeklies appear to allow more creative freedom [than dailies] because of the radicalism of much of the form and content of their comics and cartoons. But in some ways they are even worse in their culture of hypocrisy, and this includes editors . . . who expect cartoonists to 'take dictation.' " One editor would sometimes play cartoonist, supplying Wagner with ideas to execute. Wagner faced more barriers when he proposed his own concepts, such as a cartoon in 1991 about clueless cops in nearby Milwaukee who did not take seriously a complaint by a kidnap victim—a fourteen-year-old gay Asian boy—who had escaped from serial killer Jeffrey Dahmer. The police delivered the dazed, bleeding, naked boy back to Dahmer, who convinced them his prey was actually his nineteen-year-old drunk lover and that the couple had fought during a lovers' spat. In later conversations with dispatchers, reported the *Washington Post*, the police officers who left the soon-to-be crime scene were "calling the incident 'a boyfriend-boyfriend thing' and cracking jokes about getting themselves 'deloused.' "

Though Wagner allows that dailies and alternative weeklies usually espouse different politics, he thinks both lack much conviction. "I think the dailies have a history of being more honest about their capitalist imperative, where the weeklies . . . hang onto the pretense of somehow being above mere profit motive." In his experience, the progressivism of alternative weeklies is rote, motivated more by profit than social justice. "*City Pages*' all-white, all-male editors in chief during the ten years I was there would write at length about the plight of African Americans while hardly ever hiring any, and pretend to be feminists while supporting a large part of their business with porn and stripper ads."

PETE WAGNER

Killed by *City Pages*, 1991

SELF-CENSORSHIP 101

In recent years, many U.S. corporations such as Delta Airlines, American Express, and IBM have outsourced call centers to India, where operators, who sometimes struggle with English, process reservations, answer billing questions, and provide technical support. This is just one of the most obvious examples of corporate outsourcing, a practice that conservatively costs 300,000 American workers per year their jobs.

In 2004, editors of the *Missourian*, a daily newspaper in Columbus owned by the University of Missouri, handed cartoonist Joshua Eiserike what seemed like a plum assignment: satirize the phenomenon of outsourcing. The paper's editorial page, which emulates the comedic tone of *The Daily Show*, "outsourced" its columns and cartoon for one day. Eiserike "hired" Sajmeer Patel, "a fourteen-year-old Indian boy with poor knowledge of English," as a surrogate cartoonist. In reality, Eiserike "outsourced" the cartoon to his left hand.

The *Missourian*'s editors—professional journalists who were apparently influenced by the must-not-offend-anyone atmosphere sweeping America's campuses—did not get the joke. They spiked Eiserike's cartoon for being insensitive to Indians. It was not the cartoonist's first run-in with political correctness gone wild. When Eiserike drew a regular comic strip for the *Diamondback*, the newspaper of the University of Maryland, he cracked a tepid joke about Jewish mothers during "Jewish Awareness Month." The president of the Campus Jewish Student Union called for Eiserike's firing, and reported the cartoonist—a Jew himself—to the Anti-Defamation League.

In response, the *Diamondback* allotted space for the president of the Jewish student organization to condemn the cartoonist in print and allowed a response from Eiserike, who wrote: "Through humor, I've inadvertently expressed views that are rooted in race/religion and deviate from the 'sensitive' norm. Therefore, I am obviously anti-Semitic! We use this term and other labels freely for any idea presented that does not bear the hand-stamped approval of the Sensitivity Police."

Eiserike was lucky. His editors resisted pressure to fire him. Acton Gordon, the editor in chief of the University of Illinois newspaper *The Daily Illini*, was not so fortunate after he published six of the infamous Danish Mohammed cartoons to accompany his own column about the *intoonfadah*. "People wanted to see the images so they could decide for themselves if they thought they were cartoons worth killing people over," Gordon later told the *Chicago Tribune*. The local Muslim community protested Gordon's decision, and he was promptly suspended and fired—teaching journalists in training a chilling lesson.

JOSH EISERIKE

Killed by the *Missourian*, 2004

This comic strip has been outsourced to Sajmeer Patel, Age 14, India

THE GAG REFLEX

Having drawn more than 23,700 "gags," each numbered and logged in 119 three-ring binders, Sam Gross wastes little time mourning his killed cartoons. But he admittedly cherished the cartoon (page 232), bought—then rejected—by *The New Yorker*. Speaking in a saccharine-laced tone, Gross speculates that his editors may have changed their minds because he "picked on poor people from the Middle East trying to make a living."

Gross envies comedians on TV, who, in his opinion, enjoy more latitude to offend than cartoonists do. "It doesn't faze David Letterman [performing] a cabdriver gag. You can get away with more verbally than in print. The verbal goes. The print stays. 'Dear CBS, David Letterman said . . . what did he say now? But 'Dear *New Yorker* magazine, I take exception to this cartoon because the caption [says]: I hit him in the head with a chicken.' "

Gross thinks cartoons "frighten" some magazine editors. He recalls being summoned into the offices of *Good Housekeeping* by unnerved editors because one of his cartoons infuriated cat lovers. "I did this gag with four vending machines. One was a Fruit-o-matic, one was sandwiches, one was sodas, and one [dispensed] kittens." And they got letters like crazy. 'How could you put kittens in there?' "

"They brought me into this room with this pile of letters," continues Gross. "They said, 'You've got to answer these.' I said, 'You've gotta be out of your mind!' They were paying $160 [a cartoon] at the time, and I'm going to sit there and write letters? But that was the last sale I made to them."

SAM GROSS

Killed by *The New Yorker*, undated

"FROM EARTH? NO KIDDING? MY SON IS A TAXICAB DRIVER IN NEW YORK CITY."

5
PROTECTION RACKET

CORPORATE POWER AT WORK

BUTT OUT

Some editors snuff out cartoons as if they were spent cigarettes. Cartoonist Rex Babin says his former editor at the *Albany Times Union* usually wasn't one of them. "Generally," says Babin, "when you get cartoons killed, it's a sign of an unhealthy relationship with your editor, and the fact is that I had a very healthy relationship, because he encouraged me to do cartoons that push the envelope."

Babin, now at the *Sacramento Bee*, seemingly pushed the envelope too far when he drew a cartoon criticizing big tobacco's hardball negotiating tactics during settlement talks with several state governments. "I ended up drawing it too well," suggests Babin, who recalls that his editor feared upsetting sick people. "Imagine, says Babin, "someone who had a tracheotomy seeing the phalanges of the skin of the image [of the tobacco executive]."

Because he had permission to slam cigarette manufacturers with tamer imagery, Babin characterizes his editor's decision to kill the tracheotomy cartoon as "a little bit" of censorship. "If you really want to get at the tobacco companies, shouldn't you really show the result of smoking in its most graphic way?"

Big media has a long history of bowing down to big tobacco. "It's the leading cause of death and it's rarely covered," says Elizabeth M. Whelan, Sc.D., MPH, president and founder of the American Council on Science and Health, who has monitored the media's coddling of tobacco advertisers for many years. Her study of women's magazines from 1964 (the year of the first surgeon general's report linking smoking and cancer) until 1980 turned up *not a single* critical article about tobacco use in publications that accepted cigarette ads. When she held a news conference to announce the results of her study, no journalists showed up.

More recently, Whelan faults many publications for obituaries that omitted the fact that George Harrison, who succumbed to cancer in 2001 at age fifty-eight, was a longtime smoker. "Both *Time* and *Newsweek* extensively covered Harrison's death," she writes on her organization's Web site (www.acsh.org). "Coverage noted, among other details, his devotion to the Maharishi Mahesh Yogi—but neither magazine mentioned the most critical factor: cigarette smoking as the cause of death. Both magazines carry cigarette ads."

Since the 1998 settlement between tobacco companies and several states, which scaled back some advertising, there has been more coverage about the dangers of smoking, as Whelan acknowledges. But she doubts that the media can kick a habit that boosts the bottom line—although it kills off readers: "It's almost as if there's a Godfather out there keeping facts about tobacco off center stage."

REX BABIN

Killed by the *Albany Times-Union*, 1998

CAR SQUAWK

Automotive companies shelled out more than three-quarters of a billion dollars on magazine advertising during just the *first half* of 2005, and $1.2 billion on newspaper ads the year before.

Some car companies remind publishers of their V8 spending power by brazenly attempting to control the editorial content of publications in which they advertise. As Russ Baker reported in the *Columbia Journalism Review* in 1997, one auto company threatened to pull several ads in *Cosmopolitan* unless they received an advance look at a feature headlined "How to Be Very Good in Bed." A senior editor at the magazine then worked hand in driving glove with the auto company's ad agency to neuter the story. In 1996, Chrysler sent a warning letter to several magazines, demanding notification "in advance of any and all editorial content that encompasses sexual, political, social issues or any editorial that might be construed as provocative or offensive." In April 2005, General Motors cancelled its ads in the *Los Angeles Times* the day after the paper's Pulitzer Prize-winning auto critic, Dan Neil, panned the Pontiac G6. General

Motors resumed its ads five months later but delivered an unmistakable message to other publications: review at your own risk.

Some editors and publishers do not wait for Detroit to get on the phone; they hit the brakes when they think that articles or cartoons might offend car clients. In the early 1980s, not long after Milt Priggee got his first staff job at the *Dayton Journal Herald,* he got permission from his editor to draw a cartoon that bashed Detroit for making inferior compact cars. Priggee went home for the night, planning to ink his cartoon in the morning. But the publisher of the paper—which was located in a city with several auto parts factories—saw the cartoon and placed a Post-it note of rejection on the drawing.

The so-called "Chinese Wall" once insulated editors from undue business pressures, but, as Priggee points out, "if you get the publisher involved, the wall is gone."

MILT PRIGGEE

Killed by the *Dayton Journal Herald,* 1982

ALOHA, LOCAL
CARTOONISTS

From *Gentlemen's Agreement* to *All the President's Men*, Hollywood has often lionized journalists as incorruptible crusaders who do battle with entrenched powers in a quest for the truth. Although some would-be Woodwards and Bernsteins undoubtedly live up to that idealized image, a Pew survey in 2000 found that fear rather than fearlessness is the new reality in American newsrooms.

According to Pew's snapshot of self-censorship in the media, nearly three in ten reporters and editors admitted that they frequently or occasionally avoid stories that could hurt advertisers. More than one-third of the newshounds owned up to shunning stories that could damage the interests of their news organization or parent company. "Local journalists face especially difficult challenges," reported pollster Andrew Kohut in the *Columbia Journalism Review*. "Nearly one-third (32 percent) acknowledge they have softened the tone of a news story on behalf of the interests of their news organization; only 15 percent of those in the national media say they have done so."

None of this would shock cartoonist Daryl Cagle, who worked at two newspapers in Hawaii, which he describes as "a very small town." The *Honolulu Advertiser* discouraged Cagle from picking fights with local powers such as the U.S. Navy, the largest industrial employer in the state. In 2001, the *Advertiser* scuppered more than one cartoon attacking the navy after the nuclear submarine USS *Greenville* rammed a trawler carrying Japanese high school students. The sub had whooshed to the surface to wow sixteen civilian VIPs aboard—two of whom were at the *Greenville*'s helm upon impact with the *Ehime Maru*. The trawler lost nine passengers and crew. "There was another cartoonist [working] at the same time at the *Advertiser*," remembers Cagle. "I was bashing the stupid navy people for acting like asses. He was drawing leis [floating] on top of the water, and that was clearly the direction they wanted to go."

Cagle's previous employer, *Midweek*, killed many of his cartoons to spare the sensibilities of advertisers such as the Matson Navigation Company. The shipping company, which has a near-monopoly in the islands, hiked prices on Valentine's Day, eliciting a poem from Cagle (page 244). "Hawaii is entirely dependent on shipping, so Hawaii is entirely dependent on Matson," says Cagle, who notes that *Midweek* itself relied on the shipping company for deliveries of newsprint. "Criticizing Matson was not something they wanted to do."

Cagle, who runs a popular blog about the cartooning industry, foresees fewer battles of the kind he fought in Hawaii—and that troubles him. He blames the "Newsweekification" of cartoons, meaning that editors at local newspapers emulate *Newsweek*, a publication known for reprinting cartoon equivalents of superficial Jay Leno jokes instead of satire loaded with opinion. "Getting 'killed'—except for unusual circumstances—is a local phenomena, and local cartoonists are disappearing, so getting cartoons killed is kind of disappearing."

DARYL CAGLE

Killed by the *Honolulu Advertiser*, 2001

DARYL CAGLE

Killed by *Midweek*, undated

We ship all your stuff,
A very long way,
We want you to know,
That starting today,
We'll be raising your rates
And up they will stay ...

... You don't have a choice,
We know it's okay,
To squeeze you some more,
And simply to say,
We love you so much,
On Valentines Day.

THE FAIRNESS DOCTRINE

The sorry state of the American health care system sickens Dennis Draughon, formerly a cartoonist at the Pennsylvania *Scranton Times-Tribune*. As the paper's editorial page was exploring the issue of medical malpractice lawsuits, he came up with what he thought was a timely, straightforward cartoon about rising health care costs and the callous treatment of patients based on the rule of the marketplace: "Your ability to pay is as important as your need for treatment."

Draughon says his editor euthanized the cartoon, because it was perceived as "an unfair shot at doctors." Like many political cartoonists, Draughon does not seek "fairness." That subjective ideal often causes friction between cartoonists—"bomb-throwing anarchists," as Draughon refers to his ilk—and "the word folks," who are taught early and often to cherish accuracy and objectivity. "They try to come across with calm, even-measured tones and to be persuasive in that way." Visual journalists, he insists, must live by different standards, or they risk creating cartoons as limp as old lettuce. "Editorial writers have the space to opine and say 'on the other hand.' . . . An editorial cartoon is inherently unfair. A good editorial cartoon works as a gut check. It has to get in, get out, and do its dirty work real quick. You don't have time [for] 'on the other hand.' "

DENNIS DRAUGHON

Killed by the *Scranton Times-Tribune*, undated

AND CUT!

There was no major conspiracy behind the killing of Ward Sutton's cartoon about the decline of *The X-Files*. Sutton had watched in horror as the sci-fi series contrived plots to cope with the defection of disgruntled star David Duchovny. He remembers his *TV Guide* editor casually explaining, "We are trying to get Duchovny to do a cover story sometime in the future, so we are afraid we are going to offend him if we do this cartoon."

Sutton had never mistaken *TV Guide* with *Foreign Affairs*. But he considered the magazine a valuable resource. "My parents subscribed to *TV Guide*, so I read it every week," says Sutton. "Once I got a gig to work for them, I was pretty excited. All of a sudden my cousins who live in Kalamazoo would kind of understand what I do for a living."

At the time, Duchovny had sued the show's creator, Chris Carter, over money; publicly belittled his co-star, Gillian Anderson; and admitted that he phoned in some performances. So Sutton assumed his editors would want a cartoon on the topic. "I was actually commenting on something that was public discourse. I think probably any *X-Files* fan would have echoed what I was saying in this cartoon, but the fact that they were scared to print it because they didn't want to lose access to the star just showed what a sham the whole situation was. There was no journalistic integrity."

Journalistic integrity is a foreign concept to many entertainment magazines, charges an editor who has worked at several celebrity-reliant publications. The editor, who requested anonymity, decries how colleagues kowtow to Hollywood publicists. "It's a slippery slope," says the editor. "First, [publicists] want approval of the pictures, then they want approval of the words. There are places that won't grant that; they draw a line, but they are fewer and fewer." The amount of horse trading between magazines and publicists amazes the editor: "Publicists say, 'I'll give you an interview with an A-list celebrity if you do stories on my two B-list celebrities.' If you wonder why a magazine is doing a story on someone, it's because the magazine is currying favor with the publicist."

Magazines with celebrities on the cover unquestionably sell. Predicting whether to promote the career of Paris Hilton or Britney Spears has become a big part of a top editor's job. That reality, says the editor, results in "hearts and flowers" coverage of stars. The editor does see a benefit from the public's rapacious but fickle appetite for celebrity scuttlebutt, however: "The only justice is that celebrities come and go. When I was working at a women's magazine, if you got Meg Ryan on your cover, you were golden. Put Meg Ryan on your cover today and you'd sell two copies: one to Meg and another to her mother."

WARD SUTTON

Killed by *TV Guide*, 2001

ALL THE NEWS THAT'S FIT TO PRINT—UNLESS IT'S ABOUT US

The *New York Times* editorial page frequently berates the Bush White House for secrecy and subterfuge, yet the self-proclaimed "newspaper of record" sometimes fails to act with openness or accountability when its own practices come under scrutiny.

In December 2005, the *Times* revealed that the National Security Agency eavesdropped on U.S. citizens without first obtaining a warrant. It was one of the biggest stories of the year—*2004*, that is. The blockbuster briefly mentioned that editors *waited a year* before publishing the story in order to "conduct additional reporting." The suppressed scoop provoked the *Times*'s public editor, Byron Calame, to pose several questions to the paper's brain trust, including, *Was the story primarily completed before the 2004 presidential election?* In a column headlined "Behind the Eavesdropping Story, a Loud Silence," a frustrated Calame accused the *Times*'s tight-lipped editor and publisher of "stonewalling."

The *Times* is not the only paper to enforce journalistic *omerta*. According to former *Chicago Tribune* investigative reporter Geoff

Dougherty, that paper killed his analysis of 2004 executive compensation packages that reflected poorly on the performance of the Tribune Company's CEO. "Anytime you are going after ownership or people above you, there is discomfort," says Lee Judge, cartoonist at the *Kansas City Star*. "They think it's funny, and they need three copies [of the cartoon] for their friends, but they don't really want you to do it." Judge, who likens his role to that of an army sniper, has often been allowed to target his paper in print. But in 1996, Disney bought the *Star* as part of its acquisition of Capital Cities/ABC. "Disney-owned newspaper" sounded strange to Judge, as reflected by his cartoon about the deal (page 254), which the *Star* shelved. "The image [Disney] tried to portray is everything is wonderful. Life's really a fantasy. I was playing with the seamier side of life which [newspapers] represent."

Speaking of seamy, in 1988, the *Detroit Free Press* spiked more than one of Bill Day's cartoons (page 255) about Edwin Meese, Ronald Reagan's embattled attorney general. Meese was being investigated for several alleged ethical improprieties, including whether he pulled strings for a business associate who was trying to put together a billion-dollar Iraqi oil pipeline. "It looked like he was up for sale," recalls Day. But, at the time, *Free Press* executives were waiting for Meese to grant their application for a joint operating agreement with the *Detroit News*. The merging of operations (which Meese ultimately allowed before he resigned under pressure) meant massive cost savings for both papers. Day says his bosses "worried about making the guy angry. There was a lot of money involved."

Day's editor always allowed him to send rejected cartoons to a syndicate for distribution. A reporter at the *Washington Post* noticed his Meese cartoons and asked Day why they were running everywhere except Detroit. Day says that his decision to go public about the *Free Press*'s self-censorship changed his relationship with his paper (which ultimately ran the suppressed cartoons as part of a news story about the in-house controversy). "I was sweating bullets for a while. . . . But I felt I had to do it. We were pulling our punches."

LEE JUDGE

Killed by the *Kansas City Star*, 1996

A MICKEY MOUSE OPERATION

BILL DAY

Killed by the *Detroit Free Press*, 1988

YOU'RE HISTORY

The story goes that on the day in 1942 that Herb Block was hauled into the New York offices of the Newspaper Enterprise Association (NEA), he expected his syndicate to fire him. The conservative president of the NEA objected to Block's progressive politics. Yet on that very day, news broke that Block had won his first Pulitzer Prize. His job was saved.

Times have changed. In late 2005, the Tribune Company unceremoniously dumped Michael Ramirez, the Pulitzer Prize–winning cartoonist at the *Los Angeles Times*. A few weeks later, the Tribune reportedly pressured its heralded cartoonist Kevin Kallaugher, known as KAL, to accept a buyout from the *Baltimore Sun*. Both Tribune-owned papers announced that they would eliminate the position of editorial cartoonist.

The downsizing occurred during a time of impressive earnings; the Tribune Company reported an operating profit of $1.15 billion in 2005.

The Tribune Company's disregard for cartoonists—and arguably its readers—inspired "Black Ink Monday," a protest on December 12, 2005, by nearly a hundred cartoonists. According to a press release put out by the Association of American Editorial Cartoonists, their coordinated cartoons focused on "not just the loss of individual jobs but the wholesale weakening of the daily newspaper."

Unfortunately, Black Ink Monday did not get much ink. Typical was the *Tampa Tribune*, which passed on Paul Combs's protest drawing. Editors, says Combs, reasoned that their readership would not care about cartoons or about the plight of cartoonists.

The Tribune Company is not the only behemoth to cut staff during profitable times. (Despite the carping from publishers, most newspaper chains do quite nicely.) In 2003, a year in which Knight-Ridder earned a net income of $296 million, the *St. Paul Pioneer Press* laid off Kirk Anderson. Adding insult to injury, the paper refused to run Anderson's farewell cartoon (page 259), because he had circulated a memo to colleagues, excerpted below, that questioned management's priorities.

. . . I understand that difficult business decisions must be made in difficult times, and I'm glad I'm not the one who has to make those difficult decisions. But if I was . . . I'd probably cut the private service that comes in to water and dust and turn the plants in the publisher's office, before I'd cut a local cartoonist. In other words, I'd cut something only the privileged few who enter the publisher's office see, before I'd cut something 190,000 readers see. Is the position of local cartoonist really valued less than office plants?

PAUL COMBS

Killed by the *Tampa Tribune*, 2005

Paul Combs

KIRK ANDERSON

Killed by the *St. Paul Pioneer Press*, 2003

ABOUT THE EDITOR

An advocate for writers, David Wallis is the founder and editor of Featurewell.com. He has frequently lectured about the media business at Columbia University's Graduate School of Journalism, New York University, and The New School. Wallis has contributed to *The New Yorker*, *Wired*, London's *Observer*, the *Washington Post*, and the *New York Times Magazine*, among other publications. In 2004, he edited *Killed: Great Journalism Too Hot to Print*, which salon.com praised as "not just an entertaining compendium but a valuable one." He lives in the New York area.

ABOUT THE CONTRIBUTORS

Kirk Anderson was the editorial cartoonist at the *St. Paul Pioneer Press* in Minnesota from 1995 to 2003. He currently freelances his work, and is distributed by Artizans syndicate. Kirk's cartoons have been publicly denounced by a governor, officially condemned by a state university, personally admonished by a U.S. senator, reviled in print by an archbishop, and vilified by police, business leaders, talk radio hosts, the National Rifle Association, and others.

The paintings and drawings of **Marshall Arisman** have been widely published and exhibited, both internationally and nationally. His work may be seen in the permanent collections of the Brooklyn Museum, at the National Museum of American Art, and at the Smithsonian Institution. Chairman of the MFA degree program at the School of Visual Arts in New York City, Arisman was the first American invited to exhibit his artwork in mainland China. His series *Sacred Monkeys* appeared at the Guang Dong Museum of Art in April 1999.

The work of political cartoonist **Rex Babin** appears in the *Sacramento Bee* five times weekly. Babin previously was the cartoonist at the *Albany Times Union* for ten years. He was the winner of the National Press Foundation's 2001 Berryman Award and was a finalist for the 2003 Pulitzer Prize.

Sculptor and award-winning cartoonist **Khalil Bendib** is published in numerous small and mid-sized newspapers across the United States, as well as in the *Black Commentator*. Born in North Africa under a colonialist French regime, Khalil brings a fresh, non-Eurocentric perspective and a unique voice not usually found in large, corporate media. His collection *KB1—It Became Necessary to Destroy the Planet in Order to Save It* was recently published by Plan Nine Publishing.

Clay Bennett worked as a staff artist for the *Pittsburgh Post-Gazette*, and the *Fayetteville Times* in North Carolina, before accepting an editorial cartooning position with the *St. Petersburg Times* in 1981. Fired by the latter in 1994, he spent more than three years in professional oblivion before being hired as the editorial cartoonist for the *Christian Science Monitor*. He won a Pulitzer Prize in 2002.

Randy Bish has been drawing cartoons at the *Tribune-Review* in Greenburg, Pennsylvania, since 1985. His editorial cartoons have appeared in several gallery exhibits. Most recently, they have been part of two shows at the Charles Schulz Museum in California.

Herbert Block (1909–2001), known as Herblock, worked at the *Washington Post* from 1946 until his death in 2001. He won Pulitzer Prizes in cartooning in 1942, 1954, and 1979. In 1973, he was one of four staff members named in the Pulitzer Prize to the *Washington Post* for public service on Watergate.

Steve Brodner has been a satirical illustrator for nearly three decades. In 1981 he became a regular contributor to *Harper's* magazine with the monthly feature *Ars Politica*. In the 1980s, more magazines asked him to contribute regularly. His caricatures of pop and political culture have now appeared in every major publication in the United States. His most recent book is *Freedom Fries*, a political retrospective, published by Fantagraphics Books in 2004.

Daryl Cagle is the daily editorial cartoonist for msnbc.com. With more than 3 million regular, unique users each month, Daryl's editorial cartoon site with Microsoft (www.cagle.com) is the most popular cartoon Web site of any kind on the Internet. Before joining msnbc.com, Daryl was the daily political cartoonist for slate.com, Gannett's *Honolulu Advertiser*, and Hawaii's *Midweek*.

John Callahan has published six cartoon collections and an autobiography, *Don't Worry, He Won't Get Far on Foot: The Autobiography of a Dangerous Man*.

Gordon Campbell is a staff cartoonist at the *Inland Valley Daily Bulletin* in Ontario, California. In 1999 and 2003, Campbell's work brought the *Bulletin* a first place award in the California Newspaper Publishers Association's annual "Better Newspapers" contest.

In November 2002, **Rick Cole** was given the opportunity to draw a weekly cartoon for the *Trentonian* newspaper in New Jersey. He has also freelanced op-ed art for the *Philadelphia Inquirer*, cartoons for King Features Syndicate, and greeting card art for most of the major (and not-so-major) greeting card manufacturers.

Paul Combs is the editorial cartoonist for the *Tampa Tribune*. A nine-year veteran firefighter, Paul also contributes monthly cartoons to *Firehouse* magazine.

Three-time Pulitzer Prize winner **Paul Conrad** was chief editorial cartoonist of the *Los Angeles Times* from 1964 to 1993. His trenchant political observations appear in newspapers nationwide and abroad, and are syndicated four days a week by Tribune Media Services. His favorite distinction: his 1973 inclusion on Richard Nixon's enemies list. His favorite irony: Holding the Richard M. Nixon Chair at Whittier (California) College (1977–78).

A professional cartoonist since 1982, **J. D. Crowe** joined the staff of the *Mobile Register* as the daily editorial cartoonist in 2000. To paraphrase a late *Register* editorial writer, he likens his job to "kickin' over slop jars." His most recent book is *2005 Hurricane Season: A Graphic Documentary Featuring the Katrina Cartoons.*

The work of humorous illustrator **John Cuneo** appears in many national publications, including *Esquire*, *Rolling Stone*, and *Atlantic Monthly*. His first book, *nuErotic*, was published by Fantagraphics Books.

Matt Davies, the cartoonist at the *Journal News* in White Plains, New York, won the Pulitzer Prize in 2004 for "piercing cartoons on an array of topics, drawn with a fresh, original style."

Bill Day is political cartoonist for the *Memphis Commercial Appeal.* Previously, he worked at the *Detroit Free Press.* Day, the recipient of five Robert F. Kennedy Awards, won the Green Eyeshade Award from the Society of Professional Journalists in 2000. His work is widely reprinted in major national magazines, including *Newsweek, Time,* and *Business Week.*

The cartoonist known only as **Derf** sold his first cartoon, a nude portrait of his sixth grade teacher, to a classmate, who used it for unspeakable purposes. Today his comic strip, *The City*, is one of the most widely read alternative cartoons, appearing regularly in more than fifty publications.

From 1989 to 2004, **Dennis Draughon** was the staff editorial cartoonist for the *Times-Tribune* newspapers in Scranton, Pennsylvania. His work there earned a Fischetti Award for Distinguished Achievement in 1993 and the Association of American Editorial Cartoonists' 1999 Golden Spike award for the best cartoon killed by an editor. In 2005, Draughon returned to North Carolina, where he grew up. His work now appears regularly in the *Durham News* and the *Fayetteville Observer.*

Ernest Dumas was a political reporter and editorial writer for the now defunct *Arkansas Gazette* and currently writes a column for the *Arkansas Times.*

Joshua Eiserike is a three-time regional winner of the Society of Professional Journalists' Mark of Excellence Award for editorial cartooning. After a stint at Marvel Comics and completing his masters in journalism at the University of Missouri, Eiserike currently writes features and entertainment stories for the *Potomac News* in Woodbridge, Virginia.

On December 15, 1980, **Bob Englehart** joined the *Hartford Courant* as the first full-time editorial cartoonist in the history of the country's oldest newspaper, founded in 1764.

George Fisher (1923–2003) won two Bronze Stars during World War II. He continued to show bravery upon his return to his native Arkansas. His cartoons, which appeared regularly in the *Arkansas Gazette* from 1972 until the paper's demise in 1991, battled powerful interests in the South, including—but not limited to—segregationists, pro-lifers, and the National Rifle Association. His work is collected in *The Best of Fisher: 28 Years of Editorial Cartoons from Faubus to Clinton* (University of Arkansas Press).

Born in Moscow in 1972, **Roman Genn** was two years old when his parents sent him to the "toddler gulag"—four years, five days a week, twenty-four hours a day in a Communist indoctrination camp. That's where he learned to draw sadistic renderings of the other inmates and wardens. After Genn was discovered cartooning on the streets of Moscow, he emigrated to America in 1991. He serves as a contributing editor at *National Review* but also contributes to "lefty" publications such as the *Washington Post* and the *New York Times*.

Steve Greenberg is an editorial cartoonist and graphic artist for the *Ventura County Star* in Southern California. His cartoons have won awards nearly every year of his career; they have been reprinted in many of the nation's top newspapers and in sixty books.

The work of **Sam Gross** frequently appears in *The New Yorker*. Gross was the cartoon editor of *National Lampoon* and *Parents* magazine. His collections include *More Gross*, *An Elephant Is Soft and Mushy*, and *Your Mother Is a Remarkable Woman*.

Born in 1939 in Ludwigshafen, Germany, **Rainer Hachfeld** has lived in Berlin since 1952. He regularly contributes political cartoons to Cartoonists & Writers Syndicate and *Neues Deutschland*, as well as *Le Monde* and *Courier International*.

Clayton Hanmer (CTON) has worked with the *Globe & Mail*, the *Walrus*, the *Progressive*, and *Cracked* magazine, to name but a few.

Al Hirschfeld (1903–2003), arguably the greatest caricaturist of the twentieth century, long contributed to the Arts and Leisure section of the *New York Times*, as well as *Time* magazine, *TV Guide*, and *Playbill*. The Library of Congress and museums including the Museum of the City of New York and the Smithsonian Institution have exhibited Hirschfeld's art.

Lee Judge has been the cartoonist at the *Kansas City Star* since 1981.

Harry Katz is former head curator of the Prints and Photographs Division at the Library of Congress. He is the curator of the Herb Block Foundation Collection and author of several books on American cartooning. Katz is the editor of *Cartoon America: Comic Art at the Library of Congress*, a copublication of Harry N. Abrams and the Library of Congress.

Mike Keefe has been the editorial cartoonist for the *Denver Post* since 1975. He is also a weekly contributor to *USA Today*. Nationally syndicated, his cartoons have appeared in *Time*, *Newsweek*, and *Business Week* and in more than two hundred newspapers across the country, including the *New York Times* and the *Washington Post*.

Steve Kelley began his career at the *San Diego Union-Tribune* and joined the *Times-Picayune* in New Orleans in 2002. His editorial cartoons are distributed to newspapers by Creators Syndicate.

Keith Knight is an award-winning San Francisco cartoonist and rapper whose work can be seen in such varied publications as salon.com, the *Funny Times*, blacknews.com, and *Mad* magazine. His two weekly comic strips, the *K Chronicles* and *(th)ink*, can be found in more than thirty-five alternative, ethnic, political, and college newspapers across the country.

The photocollages of **Stephen Kroninger** have graced the cover of *Time* magazine, been the subject of a one-person show at the Museum of Modern Art, and been credited with sowing the seeds of the collage renaissance. For years, he did a weekly political cartoon for the *Village Voice* and taught illustration at the School of Visual Arts. His work is part of the permanent collection at the Museum of Modern Art and the National Portrait Gallery of the Smithsonian Institute.

Anita Kunz has produced cover art for many magazines, including *Rolling Stone*, *The New Yorker*, *Sports Illustrated*, and *Time* magazine. She has also illustrated more than fifty book jacket covers. Anita frequently lectures and teaches workshops at universities and institutions internationally, including the Smithsonian and the Corcoran, in Washington, D.C. Her works are in the permanent collections at the Library of Congress, the Musée Militaire de France in Paris, and the Museum of Contemporary Art in Rome. Anita was recently named one of the fifty most influential women in Canada by the *National Post* newspaper.

The illustrations and comics of **Peter Kuper** appear regularly in *Time*, *Newsweek*, the *New York Times*, and *Mad* magazine, where he illustrates SPY vs. SPY every month. His most recent books are adaptions of Franz Kafka's *The Metamorphosis* and Upton Sinclair's *The Jungle* and *Sticks and Stones*.

Carol Lay has drawn comics and illustrations for many publications including *Mad* magazine, the *Wall Street Journal*, and *The New Yorker*. Her weekly comic strip can be seen on salon.com and at www.waylay.com.

M. G. Lord was a columnist and political cartoonist at *New York Newsday*. Her most recent book is *Astro Turf: The Private Life of Rocket Science* (Walker & Co.).

Born in Dunedin, New Zealand, **David Low** (1891–1963) achieved success as a cartoonist while a teenager. In 1919, he was recruited by England's *Daily News* and the company's evening paper, the *Star*. Conservative press baron Lord Beaverbrook convinced him to jump to the *Evening Standard*, where Low warned Britons about the threat of fascism before it was fashionable. Low's books include *A Cartoon History of the War*, *Low's Company*, *Low's Autobiography*, and *Years of Wrath: 1932–1945*.

Mike Luckovich, of the *Atlanta Journal-Constitution*, received the top honor of his profession when he won the Pulitzer Prize for editorial cartooning in 1995 and 2005. Luckovich's cartoons, syndicated nationally by Creators Syndicate, appear in more than 350 daily publications.

Graeme MacKay grew up in Dundas, Ontario, Canada. He has always been a "news geek," and was the kid who never stopped doodling. He is the full-time editorial cartoonist for the *Hamilton Spectator*.

Born in Greensboro, North Carolina, **Doug Marlette** began drawing political cartoons for the *Charlotte Observer* in 1972. He joined the

Atlanta Journal-Constitution in 1987, *New York Newsday* in 1989, the *Tallahassee Democrat* in 2002, and the *Tulsa World* in 2006. He won the Pulitzer Prize in 1988.

R. J. Matson is the editorial cartoonist for the *St. Louis Post-Dispatch*. He also draws one cartoon a week for the *New York Observer* and four cartoons a week for *Roll Call* when Congress is in session.

Hal Mayforth started his illustration career in Boston and returned to his native Vermont, where he lives with his wife and three sons. Hal has been the recipient of many awards and honors, including Cartoonist of the Year by the National Cartoonists Society in 1993 and a swimming award at Camp Abnaki in the early 1960s. His illustration clients include *Time*, *Newsweek*, the *Wall Street Journal*, *Outside*, *Sports Illustrated*, Coke, Pepsi, and HBO.

The elder daughter of **Terry Mosher** is named Aislin, the nom de plume that Mosher has used for more than thirty years as the editorial page cartoonist for Montreal's English-language newspaper, the *Gazette*. To date, thirty-eight Aislin books have been published. The most recent collection—entitled *OH, OH!*—covers the momentous period between September 11, 2001, and the June 2004 Canadian federal election.

Tim O'Brien creates intricately detailed illustrations and portraits, which can be seen in *Time*, *Esquire*, the *Atlantic Monthly*, *Rolling Stone*, *National Geographic*, and many other publications. Additional clients include book publishers such as HarperCollins, Penguin, Scholastic, Inc., and Simon & Schuster, and a wide variety of advertising agencies. Tim is a founding member of the Illustrators' Partnership of America. He is on the Illustration Advisory Board of the Norman Rockwell Museum, and is currently the vice president of the Society of Illustrators and the chairman of its scholarship competition.

Patrick O'Connor is the editorial cartoonist at the *Los Angeles Daily News*. He is the winner of several awards, including the 1998 John Locher Memorial Award.

Mel Odom has exhibited his work in group shows at the Cooper-Hewitt Museum in New York City and the Society of Illustrators. In 1989, *Playboy* named him Illustrator of the Year.

Joel Pett, winner of the 2000 Pulitzer Prize for editorial cartooning, has been the editorial cartoonist at the *Lexington Herald Leader* since 1984. His cartoons have appeared in hundreds of newspapers and magazines, including the *New York Times*, the *Washington Post*, and the *Los Angeles Times*. Pett's cartoon collections are available in four paperback books, the latest being *Just Don't Inhale*.

After college, **Milt Priggee** met his mentor, John Fischetti, in Chicago. Fischetti helped Priggee start freelancing. The *Dayton Journal Herald* hired Priggee in July 1982. When the newspaper ceased publication in 1986, Priggee landed at the *Spokesman-Review* in Spokane, Washington, in February 1987. Currently he is self-syndicated from his base in Oak Harbor, Washington, where he continues to produce cartoons on local, national, and world topics.

A Pulitzer Prize finalist in 1996, **Ted Rall** has published four books and three collections of cartoons. Most recently, he edited *Attitude: The New Subversive Political Cartoonists*, a ground-breaking cartoon collection of alternative cartoonists, and *To Afghanistan and Back*, the first-ever instant graphic travelogue, which chronicles Ted's harrowing experiences covering the war for the *Village Voice* and KFI Radio. His work is syndicated by Universal Press Syndicate.

Mikhaela Reid is a twenty-five-year-old political cartoonist for the *Boston Phoenix* and *Bay Windows*. Her work has also appeared in *Ms.*, the *Los Angeles Times*, and *Metro Times Detroit*.

Dennis Renault was the staff cartoonist for the *Sacramento*, *Fresno*, and *Modesto Bee*s from 1971 until 1999. He has been awarded the prize for the best editorial cartoons in the state by the California Newspaper Publishers Association, and has received the Overseas Press Club's Citation for Excellence and the H. L. Mencken Award.

In 1916, **Norman Rockwell** (1894–1978) painted the first of 321 covers for the *Saturday Evening Post*. In 1963, he left the *Post* and started a ten-year association with *Look* magazine. In 1977, Jimmy Carter awarded Rockwell the Presidential Medal, the nation's highest civilian honor. To learn more about Rockwell's legacy, visit www.nrm.org.

Flash Rosenberg is a photographer, cartoonist, writer, performer, teacher, romantic, and turtle wrangler. Her cartoons, essays, and illustrations have appeared in the *New York Times*, the *Wall Street Journal*, the *Forward*, the *Funny Times*, and *Lilith*, as well as in numerous cartoon compendiums, including *Life's a Stitch: The Best of Contemporary Women's Humor*.

Phil Somerville was born in Sydney, Australia, in 1954 to musician parents. Schooled at a private boys' Catholic college, he graduated to gain employment at the afternoon tabloid the *Daily Mirror*. He aspired to written journalism but was sacked as a copyboy after three years for "unethical and undisclosed use of company resources for purposes of libelous commentary upon higher staff members by way of a secretly published parody newspaper within the greater company premises of News Ltd." His first commentary cartoons appeared weekly for almost two years in the premier broadsheet *Sydney Morning Herald* starting in 1986. He picked up weekly spots in that newspaper again from 1997 to 2003. He has had one book collection of his cartoons published in 2001 titled *I am moderately fond of Australia* (HardieGrant, Melbourne).

Edward Sorel is a regular contributor to the *Atlantic* and *The New Yorker.* Besides his dozens of covers for the latter, his art has appeared on the covers of *Harper's*, *Fortune*, *Forbes*, and the *Nation*, among other publications. He has illustrated many children's books, three of which he also wrote. *Unauthorized Portraits* (Knopf, 1997) is the most recent of several collections of his work. In 2001, the Art Directors Club of New York elected him to their Hall of Fame, the first cartoonist since John Held, Jr., to be so honored.

While his sixth grade teacher looked the other way, **Ward Sutton** began honing his comic art skills and has been expanding the scope of his work ever since. His self-syndicated weekly comic strip, *Schlock'n'Roll*, debuted in 1995. His cartoons have appeared in *TV Guide*, *Rolling Stone*, the *New York Times*.

Paul Szep, formerly editorial cartoonist for the *Boston Globe*, has won two Pulitzer Prizes. Since retiring from the *Globe* in 2001, Szep's work is now featured regularly in numerous publications, including the *St. Petersburg Times*.

During his career in publishing, **J. P. Trostle** has been an art director, an illustrator, a graphic designer, a writer, an editor, and—last but not least—a cartoonist, most recently for the *Herald-Sun* in Durham, North Carolina. He is also the current editor of the *Notebook*, the quarterly magazine of the Association of American Editorial Cartoonists.

Garry Trudeau is the creator of *Doonesbury*. In 1975, he won the Pulitzer Prize, the first comic artist to do so.

Pete Wagner has been drawing political cartoons for alternative and college newspapers since 1970. He was staff cartoonist for *City Pages*, the major weekly in Minneapolis, for ten years. Wagner now teaches a political cartooning course at the Minneapolis College of Art and Design. His work can be found online at www.wagtoons.com.

ACKNOWLEDGMENTS

When my literary agent left the industry without warning, Andrew Blauner jumped in, rescued this book, and found it a fine home. He has my sincerest thanks. I greatly enjoyed collaborating with the delightful Amy Cherry of W. W. Norton, who consistently championed the project. Lucinda Bartley, who will have an impressive career in publishing, also deserves my thanks. The wise counsel of my mentor, Gerald Jonas, proved as invaluable as ever. My friends Abby Ellin, Amy Alkon, Daniel Asa Rose, Gretchen Primack, Jessica Seigel, Robert Sawyer, RaNae Merrill, and Stanley Mieses read parts of the manuscript and answered my panicked calls at all hours. Sam Gross, Edward Sorel, Dennis Draughon, Steve Brodner, Ted Rall, J. P. Trostle, Ruth Marten, David Flaherty, and Ellen Weinstein taught me about cartooning and illustration. Sylvia Rhor, of the Andy Warhol Museum, who curated "Too Hot to Handle: Creating Controversy Through Political Cartoons," gave generously of her time and resources. Alex Rawls chipped in when I most needed it, conducting several important interviews as my deadline approached. My gratitude also goes to R. C. Harvey; David Friedman; Roman Genn; David Levine; Mirko Ilic; Kellie Menger; Stewart Hawkins; Lisa Hyman; Dr. Tim Benson; Todd DePastino; Luke Warm; Peter Sis; Ernest Dumas; Harry Katz; David Leopold; Steve Heller; Fredrick Voss; Cathy Seipp; Susan Shapiro; Charlie Rubin; John Rockwell; Linda Pero, of the Norman Rockwell Museum; the Herb Block Foundation; and the New York Public Library.

Anyone with an interest in cartooning should also read Christopher Lamb's *Drawn to Extremes: The Use and Abuse of Editorial Cartoons in the United States* and *Drawn and Quartered: The History of American Political Cartoons*, by Stephen Hess and Sandy Northrop.

Finally, much love to my family: Mom, Dad, Stephen, Sarah, Sofia Jade, Lenny, Glo, and Marilyn. Without my wife, Penny, I would be lost. Thanks for putting up with me during the two years it took me to finish this book.

CREDITS

CREDITS

p. 76: Copyright 2005 Clayton Hanmer. Reprinted with permission of Clayton Hanmer.

p. 81: Copyright Doug Marlette. Reprinted with permission of Doug Marlette. Published in *In Your Face: A Cartoonist at Work* (New York: Houghton Mifflin, 1991).

p. 82: Copyright Doug Marlette. Reprinted with permission of Doug Marlette. Published in *In Your Face: A Cartoonist at Work* (New York: Houghton Mifflin, 1991).

p. 87: Copyright 2006 Randy Bish. Reprinted with permission of Randy Bish.

p. 90: Copyright 2005 Khalil Bendib. Reprinted with permission of Khalil Bendib.

p. 94: Copyright 2006 R. J. Matson. Reprinted with permission of R. J. Matson.

p. 95: Copyright 2006 R. J. Matson. Reprinted with permission of R. J. Matson.

p. 98: Copyright 2005 Bob Englehart. Reprinted with permission of Bob Englehart.

p. 99: Copyright 2005 Randy Bish. Reprinted with permission of Randy Bish.

p. 100: Copyright 2002 Kirk Anderson. Reprinted with permission of Kirk Anderson.

p. 103: Copyright 2005 Graeme MacKay. Reprinted with permission of Graeme MacKay.

p. 104: Copyright 2005 J. D. Crowe. Reprinted with permission of J. D. Crowe.

p. 106: Copyright 1996 Flash Rosenberg. Reprinted with permission of Flash Rosenberg.

p. 110: Copyright 1993 Bob Englehart. Reprinted with permission of Bob Englehart.

p. 113: Copyright 1972 Paul Szep. Reprinted with permission of Paul Szep.

p. 120: Copyright 1937 David Low. Reprinted with permission of Solo Syndication/Associated Newspapers.

p. 123: Copyright 1952 Herbert Block. Reprinted with permission of the Herb Block Foundation.

p. 126: Copyright George Fisher. Published in *The Best of Fisher: 28 Years of Editorial Cartoons from Faubus to Clinton*. Reprinted with permission of the University of Arkansas Press.

p. 129: Copyright 1993 Dennis Renault. Reprinted with permission of Dennis Renault.

p. 132: Copyright Marshall Arisman. Reprinted with permission of Marshall Arisman.

p. 136: Copyright 1985 G. B. Trudeau. Reprinted with permission of United Press Syndicate. All rights reserved.

p. 137: Copyright 1985 G. B. Trudeau. Reprinted with permission of United Press Syndicate. All rights reserved.

p. 138: Copyright M.G. Lord. Reprinted with permission of M.G. Lord.

p. 139: Copyright 2006 Mikhaela Reid. Reprinted with permission of Mikhaela Reid.

p. 142: Copyright 2001 Stephen Kroninger. Reprinted with permission of Stephen Kroninger.

p. 145: Copyright 1998 Ted Rall. Reprinted with permission of Ted Rall.

p. 146: Copyright 1980 Mel Odom. Reprinted with permission of Mel Odom.

p. 147: Copyright 1987 Milt Priggee. Reprinted with permission of Milt Priggee.

p. 150: Copyright 1988 Steve Brodner. Reprinted with permission of Steve Brodner.

p. 154: Copyright 2000 Ward Sutton. Reprinted with permission of Ward Sutton.

p. 155: Copyright 2000 Ward Sutton. Reprinted with permission of Ward Sutton.

CREDITS

CREDITS